RETHINKING FAMILY-SCHOOL RELATIONS:
A CRITIQUE OF PARENTAL INVOLVEMENT
IN SCHOOLING

Sociocultural, Political, and Historical Studies in Education
Joel Spring, Editor

RETHINKING FAMILY–SCHOOL RELATIONS: A CRITIQUE OF PARENTAL INVOLVEMENT IN SCHOOLING

Maria Eulina P. de Carvalho

Universidade Federal da Paraíba, Brazil

LEA
2001

LAWRENCE ERLBAUM ASSOCIATES, PUBLISHERS
Mahwah, New Jersey   London

Extracts used throughout this volume were taken from the following sources:

From "Cultural reproduction and social reproduction in Knowledge, education and cultural change," by P. Bourdieu, 1977. In J. Karabel & A. H. Halsey (Eds.), *Power and ideology in education*, pp. 487–511). New York: Oxford University Press. Reprinted with permission.

From *Reproduction in education, society, and culture* by P. Bourdieu & J.-C. Passerson, Beverly Hills, CA: Sage. Copyright © 1977 by Sage. Reprinted with permission.

From "The forms of capital" by P. Bourdieu, 1986. In J. G. Richardson (Ed.), *Handbook of theory and research for the sociology of education*. New York, Westport CT, London: Greenwood Press. Reprinted with permission.

From "Equal Schools for Equal Students," by James S. Coleman, 1966, *The Public Interest*, 4, pp. 70–75. Copyright © 1999 by National Affairs, Inc. Reprinted with permission of the author.

From "Toward Open Schools," by James S. Coleman, 1967, *The Public Interest*, 9, pp. 20–27. Copyright © 1999 by National Affairs, Inc. Reprinted with permission of the author.

The final camera copy for this work was prepared by the author, and therefore the publisher takes no responsibility for consistency or correctness of typographical style. However, this arrangement helps to make publication of this kind of scholarship possible.

Lawrence Erlbaum Associates, Inc., Publishers
10 Industrial Avenue
Mahwah, NJ 07430

Cover design by Kathryn Houghtaling Lacey

Library of Congress Cataloging-in-Publication Data

de Carvalho, Maria Eulina P.
Rethinking family–school relations : a critique of parental involvement in schooling / Maria Eulina P. de Carvalho.
p.   cm. — (Sociocultural, political, and historical studies in education)
Includes bibliographical references and index.
ISBN 0-8058-3496-6 (cloth : alk. paper) — ISBN)-8058-3957-7 (pbk. : Alk. paper)
1. Home and school. 2. Education—Parent participation. I. Title. II. Series.
LC225 .D259   2000
370.19'2—dc21

00-026748
CIP

Books published by Lawrence Erlbaum Associates are printed on acid-free paper, and their bindings are chosen for strength and durability.

Printed in the United States of America
10 9 8 7 6 5 4 3 2 1

Contents

Prologue

School doors open for parents to help.
Just a little involvement can boost education.

This was the headline of an article in the *Detroit Free Press*, August 25, 1997 (Van Moorlehem, 1997). According to the article, boosting education is all a matter of parental sentiment and time, presented as a "simple and inexpensive act" (p. 1-A). And there is "a ton of research" (p. 1-A) recommending parental involvement—not just at home but at school—as the remedy schools and students need most at this moment. Impediments to parental involvement are reduced to parents' timidity, uneasiness at school, time constraints, and lack of encouragement from teenagers, which can be reversed by school personnel's openness and warmth, and the provision of a range of opportunities for parents. In addition to involvement in traditional fund-raising, help at special classes, sports, bands, academic clubs, and parties, participation is now invited in school governance, curriculum, and budgeting.

Needs and benefits of parental involvement are amply depicted, based on current research findings. Teachers need parents, therefore the partnership idea combines teachers' expertise in child development and curriculum with parents' expertise about their own children. Young children, in particular, benefit from getting a sense that the whole family is a part of school when their parents are around, but "middle and high school students, and the schools themselves, need parents as much as the elementary ones do" (Van Moorlehem, 1997, p. 1-A). The older students need parental guidance through academic choices in order to take the right courses and tests to get into college.

The role of parents in face of the growing complexity of homework is also acknowledged, with emphasis on the need to be supportive rather than doing the student's homework: "Thankfully you don't have to remember your high school algebra to be a good parent. More important than helping solve individual algebraic problems is encouraging students to stick with a subject that is tough, but that will expand their range of career and life choices" (Van Moorlehem, 1997, p. 1-A).

Parents, in turn, benefit from networking with other parents and families. And the whole family benefits: Because school is the main external influence in children's lives, parental involvement in schooling builds family cohesion, as parents develop a common language with their children. Moreover, parental involvement

1

should be fun, as in the case of math and science carnivals. Examples of exceptionally involved parents are presented in the article, typically a father who participates in the evening, while his wife, "a stay-at-home mom, pitches in at school during the day" (Van Moorlehem, 1997, p. 1-A). The message for "parents with jobs" is that they "will have to be more creative" (p. 1-A).

As just evidenced, parental involvement as a policy strategy appears as a peculiar response to a host of school and family issues, promising improvement for schools and families, and combining institutional and individual goals, that is, gains in school productivity and student success. The fact that it has become a national educational goal, in President Clinton's 1994 Goals 2000: Educate America Act, is suggestive of its rhetorical power in synthesizing cultural expectations and values related to the current sense of crisis in both the institutions of school and family. As Casanova (1996) noted, "the value of parental involvement has become an acceptable truism across a wide spectrum of political positions in the U.S. Conservatives and liberals, religious fundamentalists and secular families have all endorsed parental involvement as a fundamental component of successful schooling" (p. 30). However, it is important to distinguish between parental involvement in education as a desirable attitude and practice of individual parents, in the interest of their children's school success, and parental involvement as a policy strategy designed to promote it where it appears lacking, and as a formal incentive aiming at enhancing school outcomes in an indirect way in the name of democratic opportunity.

In fact, as Casanova (1996) cautioned, the meaning of parental involvement is neither consensual nor is its practice necessarily positive, leading sometimes to undesirable excesses on the part of parents (as individuals or organized groups), with negative consequences for children, teachers, and the school community. Nevertheless, the general policy formula espouses a very romanticized view of education and family–school relations. It encloses and conceals different parental role constructions and levels of involvement related to both family and school particular contexts and practices, as well as potential conflicts in family–school and teacher–parent relations, and even among parents, associated with diversity of social class, ethnicity, family organization, and values.

In Epstein's (1992, 1995) model, for instance, levels of parental involvement range from involvement in the home (attending to basic needs, disciplining, preparing for school, supporting school learning, and/or engaging actively in homework) to participation in school activities and events, but playing the role of teacher-aide (volunteering in the classroom and/or tutoring homework), and participating in school decision making are considered higher (and more desirable) levels of parental involvement toward the ideal of integration of family, community, and school resources. This model, however, is based on a small number of actual successful school–family–community partnerships and on the characteristics of the already positively involved parents and communities, and their schools.

Accordingly, the general policy formula furthers one particular model of parental involvement in education and schooling, judged positive from the school's perspective (according to which successful schooling is, indeed, dependent on parental input), apparently aiming at counteracting parental apathy (defined as a discrete problem), while ignoring the very dynamics of differentiation across schools and families, of more or less subtle power struggles between parents and educators (Henry, 1996), and of ambivalence in teachers' views (Smrekar, 1996). In seeking to generalize such a model, the policy neglects the various and complex reasons why a majority of parents are not involved in the terms or degrees expected by schools and teachers in the first place. It also overlooks the implications of mandated and enhanced parental involvement for schools as organizations, teachers' work, family life (especially in the case of those families and parents perceived as noninvolved), and the democratic equality purpose of the public school (Labaree, 1997).

   Negative effects of the policy and practice of parental involvement have already been evidenced. A general effect may be reinforcing patterns of discrimination based on social class, ethnicity, and gender through the creation of new stratified structures of participation, with lower class and minority mothers helping in the school cafeteria, for instance, while upper-middle class mothers and fathers act as classroom volunteers and school council members. The specific policing role attributed to parents in monitoring teachers' activities and in controlling the curriculum and budget, on the other hand, is not only likely to undermine trust and enhance animosity between teachers and parents, but also to set groups of parents in competition for influence over school policies, with antidemocratic consequences (Casanova, 1996; Henry, 1996; Smrekar, 1996).

   Casanova's (1996) "call for prudence" (p. 30) regarding parental involvement takes the perspective of the school and teacher professionalism. In accordance with R. T. Ogawa (cited in Casanova, 1996), Casanova poses both the need to create bridges—because schools "are dependent on parents to provide resources that affect the academic performance of their students"—and buffers—"to protect the school from interference with the professional discretion of teachers and principals" (p. 31). In this way, she retrieved the protective model of family–school relations (Swap, 1993), pointing out that what needs to be protected is the "national interest" and "the greater good" against "parochial considerations" (p. 32). In contrast, most of the discourse (of policy and research) exalts the school–family partnership ideal, taking for granted both its desirability and viability. Although recognizing that the partnership model is hard to implement, requiring major school restructuring, Swap (1993), for instance, envisioned parent–educator collaboration to achieve the common mission of improving the school and supporting the success of all children, through two-way communication, expansion of the parent's academic role, mutual support, and joint decision making. But, in general, both the policy and research literature on the issue takes for granted the perspective of parents on family–school relations and their specific involvement in instruction, as well as the conditions of diverse families in fulfilling their appointed role in the partnership.

   I take a distinct stance regarding this matter. I am concerned with teacher's work and professional authority, with families' life conditions and parents' choices, and with educational equity, but I have doubts about the viability of the partnership model and about the justice of the mandate on parental involvement. Not that I do not find the partnership vision desirable or parental involvement in schooling, per se, as a sensible idea, but I do not see the social conditions necessary to universalize school–family partnerships in terms of equal political power in defining the curriculum, a specifically academic role for families, and shared accountability for educational outcomes. Moreover, neither do I see existing school conditions for the implementation of a range of opportunities for all parents to help schools and further all children's learning, nor do I count on parents' capability and willingness to become teachers of their own children within the frame of the school curriculum.

Therefore, I consider it fundamental to clarify why schools are dependent on parents for student success, and whether they could expand on their pedagogic role and reach their specific goals independent of family input. This requires unpacking the tacit theory of family–school relations, which informs the ideology and policy of parental involvement in schooling. Accordingly, this theory must justify both the desirability and viability of parental involvement in schooling as a general practice. Why parental involvement in schooling is necessary, both from the school and the family perspectives, precedes how (a choice of strategies) to promote it. In other words, the question of how effective this particular policy can be surely depends on the previous (theoretical) understanding.

An overview of education and family–school relations reveals two movements and concepts, which might converge or diverge: One movement in which the school is considered an (organic) extension of the family, and the other in which the family is devised (in a quite totalitarian way) as either an adversary (in a negative way) or a subsidiary (in a positive way) of the school. The first movement corresponds to the history of schooling as a middle class institution, originating from local initiative, which came to constitute the prevalent ideology of family–school relations. The second movement is related to compulsory schooling, education as acculturation or salvation for the lower classes, and requires the cultural alignment of their families to the school. While within the first movement family–school relations are unproblematic and framed in terms of positive continuity, it is only within the second movement that they become an object of explicit policy intervention.

Accordingly, from the school perspective there are two ways of seeing the family. First, the family is a resource for school achievement, and parental involvement in education in the home and school is taken for granted as natural. Second, the family is deficient and itself in need of education, and thus parental support of schooling becomes an explicit requirement for student achievement. Within this logic, family–school relations appear as essentially convergent, and school success or failure becomes a simple matter of family accountability. Hence, educational policy has tended implicitly and/or explicitly to encompass the family, ignoring the conditions of its positive contribution to schooling in the first case, and focusing on parental re-education in the second case.

An alternative view—the ideal family–school partnership—might pose the school mission in terms of embracing cultural diversity and, thus, learning from families, in which case the formula would be teacher involvement with families and school–community partnerships. For teachers, in particular, this brings up problems of choice and commitment in face of conflicting values and interests, and tensions between bureaucratic norms and individual desires. Fundamentally, there is the unsolved problem of building a common culture amid cultural pluralism. While it seems unquestionable that the school mission is to build a common and democratic culture, and while schooling has staged *cultural wars* over curriculum, this problem is curiously absent from the official discourse on parental involvement and family–school partnerships.

If schools need parents and bridges with families, and, at the same time, autonomy and discretion in defining education, as Casanova (1996) asserted, can parents' position in relation to school escape subordination? It practically can only when school is truly an extension of the family, that is, where there is cultural continuity between home and school, in which case parental involvement is natural.

However, the fact that policy is enforcing parental involvement and home–school partnerships reveals three contradictions.

First, it recognizes that parental involvement occurs neither spontaneously nor extensively. Yet, at the same time in which it calls for more parental involvement, it omits the fact that, within the liberal-meritocratic context, the benefits of parental involvement have been concretely and ultimately related to its exclusivity—that is, student success (a quantitatively limited phenomenon) has been constructed on the basis of parental involvement as a rare resource, as involvement pays off against others' noninvolvement, becoming a positive marker for teachers and influencing student evaluation (Lareau, 1993).

Second, the fact that parental involvement is considered a factor of school success suggests that instruction is organized in ways that require individual learning and reinforcement out of the school's space and time, denying the specialized (and thus exclusive) educational role of the school. Along this line, a policy enforcing parental involvement legitimizes both a particular form of learning organization and a particular path to school success, based on a particular form of family–school interaction and family contribution, a form of learning which has not worked for all students, and a path to school success which has remained narrow so far.

Third, the call for generalized parental involvement entails the assumption that it is viable. If policy effectiveness depends on likely practice, how can the promise of parental involvement be theoretically sustained? From one perspective, the fact that it has functioned (as power) for certain students and families precisely derives from its distinction (Bourdieu, 1987). What alternative perspective on family–school relations is there to inform the promise that parental involvement, granted its general possibility, could function (as power convertible in school success) for all? Such a theory is not available. Though most research on family influence on student achievement intends to be positively conclusive, it focuses either on successful interventions (compensatory programs) or favorable versus unfavorable family processes (Henderson & Berla, 1994) viewed from the school perspective, naturally corroborating the idea that parental involvement makes a difference and, thus, the cultural tradition and ideology that sustains the particular project of successful (middle-class) schooling.

On the part of schools, do they have the organizational capacity necessary to carry partnerships in the broad and democratic terms defined? Let's imagine that all parents showed up in school and demanded to volunteer in the classroom, to conference with teachers, to learn about the curriculum, to plan and discuss homework, and to participate in all levels of decision making! Imagining this picture leads to the suspicion that the call for more parental participation is a bluff.

On the part of families, what is the guarantee that parents (precisely those noninvolved) will respond positively to a policy call? An unfortunate consequence of cultural imposition may be growing alienation and resistance. Hence, because it basically depends on individual compliance, the formalization of parental involvement into a mandate, implying its acknowledgement as a legitimate resource applied to student learning and further evaluation, is likely to consecrate and increase discrimination between students of involved and noninvolved parents. And here the sad consequence is punishing students with more or less subtle pressures and, ultimately, with low grades, because of their parents' shortcomings!

In my account, the current policy focus on the family neglects three main points. First, it disregards the fact that family material and cultural conditions, and feelings about schooling differ according to social class, while proclaiming parental involvement as a means to enhance (and perhaps equalize) school outcomes. In this way, the partnership or parental involvement ideal is more likely to be a projection of the model of upper middle-class, suburban, community schooling than an open invitation for diverse families to recreate schooling. Whereas the attempt to generalize a model—produced within restricted social conditions—through a policy mandate is disputable (and its enforcement certainly oppressive), parental empowerment and participation in school reform is unlikely for the same reasons why parental involvement is found lacking—reasons derived from the organization of social (work and family) life, families' diverse cultures, and the organization and culture of schools (Valdes, 1996).

Second, although it appeals to the image of the traditional community school, the pressure for more family educational accountability really overlooks historical, as well as present social conditions. A division of educational work and content between family and school was historically constructed and is concretely maintained within the practical organization of daily life and hierarchization of social knowledge. Finally, the third important point omitted is that family–school relations are relations of power, and most families are powerless (Fine, 1993). Thus, in attempting to reach out and bring in families, this model represents a confused vision of the social function and pedagogic mission of the public school, which serves the majority and variety of social groups, as well as of the possibilities and responsibilities of families regarding school success.

Two linked effects of this policy seem the gravest, in my view: the imposition of a particular parenting style and intrusion into family life, and the escalation of educational inequality. Insofar as there are families that cannot fulfill the requisite parenting role, or create a learning environment in the home aligned to the school curriculum, the likelihood that this policy will enhance inequality of learning and outcomes seems obvious, moreover ratifying the possibility of blaming families for student failure.

This volume addresses these sorts of complications and implications of parental involvement as a policy through an exploratory theoretical approach, including historical and sociological accounts and personal reflection. It looks at some of the information that is already available and may illuminate general tendencies toward the articulation of schools, families, and educational outcomes, and at the current policy rhetoric as representative of actual or desirable practices in this camp. In short, it represents an effort to understand the origins, meanings, and effects of parental involvement as a requisite of schooling, and particularly as a policy *solution* for low achievement and even inequity in the U.S. educational scenario.

ACKNOWLEDGMENTS

The contents of this book originates from a doctoral dissertation presented to the Department of Teacher Education, at Michigan State University, in 1997. I am especially grateful to David Labaree, who found my "counter-intuitive" view on homework and family–school relations interesting, and to Steven Weiland, Doug Campbell, and Cleo Cherryholmes, who supported my work in various ways. I am also indebted to many professors and colleagues from the MSU College of Education. Among the latter, I thank the friendship of Angela Shojgreen, Fernando Cajas, and Don Hones.

While attending MSU, I was fully supported by my home university— Universidade Federal da Paraíba (UFPB), and by a scholarship from CAPES— Fundação Coordenação de Aperfeiçoamento de Pessoal do Ensino Superior, of the Brazilian Ministry of Education.

As a mother, I dedicate this work to my children, Daniel, Valentin, and Maíra, for their resilience and tolerance during the four years we lived in East Lansing, away from extended family and friends, when they had to help with the domestic work and cope with my own hectic schedules. As a single-parent, a PhD student, a person with a particular view on family–school relations, and a mother who has a life of her own, I was very little involved in their school life.

As the child I once was, I dedicate this work to my household maids, Maria, Dora, and Dona Antonia (my Black Grandmother), unschooled educators of my childhood years.

1

The Articulation of Family and School in Educational Policy

What makes a teacher spend precious time after class telephoning parents about her students' poor performance and urging parents to help her instructional efforts, instead of dealing somehow directly with those at-risk students? What are the limits of good teaching, and what—and how effectively—can parents contribute to classroom instruction?

The call for more parental participation in schooling basically acknowledges an undesirable and harmful distance between family and school, and launches an array of policy efforts to make this relationship closer. It finds ground on commonsense knowledge of a continuity of educational roles, values, and experiences between family and school, as well as on schools and teachers' expectations regarding certain learning preconditions developed in the home, and the incentives certain parents place on educational achievement.

This volume explores rationales and implications of family–school relations as defined under the current call for parental involvement, family–school partnerships, more homework, and parental education in U.S. schools. Specifically, I analyze how the educative roles of family and school, the meanings of a public school, the role and scope of educational policy toward the family, and their implications (for parents, teachers, students, and educational goals and outcomes) are framed by policy discourses and grounded by related theoretical and empirical literature.

As a framework for literary and documentary analysis, I draw on Bourdieu and Passeron's (1977) concepts of symbolic (particularly cultural) capital, and education as symbolic violence (or cultural imposition). Cultural capital, a type of embodied knowledge that functions as power within specific institutional settings, is the medium of family–school relations, and an implicit element of educational policy. As the outcome of family and class socialization, it is the (variable) medium of educational achievement, which may be exchanged for (or merely confirm previous) social and economic positions. However, cultural capital is not uniformly distributed, accessible, or produced in society.

Parental involvement, as family educational input, has been explicitly pointed out and called on as a resource for school success in recent research and policy literature in the United States (Coleman, 1991; Henderson & Berla, 1994). Conceived as a cultural role (Hoover-Dempsey & Sandler, 1997), derived from the successful model of schooling of the middle classes based on cultural continuity between home and school (that is, on family aspirations of upward social mobility via education, and on a complementary school pedagogy that requires the contribution of the family via homework), it is unquestionably seen as necessary and beneficial. The diversity of family material and cultural resources and the way specific instructional practices capitalize on them, however, have not been acknowledged except in compensatory, short-range policies. Along this line, I pose educational policy—specifically drawing on the family as a resource subordinated to the school curriculum and practices—as an important set of structures (discourses and practices) for the play of cultural capital, and hence for the exercise of symbolic violence, with contradictory effects.

Once the role of educational policy, in relation to cultural capital, is acknowledged as an instrument of symbolic violence and social (re)production, a clearer picture of the educational responsibilities, ranges, possibilities, limits, and specific articulations of school and family may be drawn. A clearer picture is needed for understanding and redefining the social purposes and possibilities of the public school, delimiting the contribution of the family in a more equitable way, and reassessing the role and implications of educational policy.

THE FAMILY AS AN OBJECT OF EDUCATIONAL POLICY

Traditionally, schools and teachers have depended on and requested family or parental collaboration. However, what has not been so evident is that family–school affinities and partnerships have had a middle-class character and a social mobility accent. Moreover, they appeared as an organic expression of the community school and of a particular stage and context of social development in which school played a central integrative role.

To be sure, families, schools, and communities have changed and grown in diversity and complexity, and so has grown the role of educational policy—grounded in research knowledge—in attempting to address the complexities and crises in school and society. In this way, parental involvement in schooling has been explicitly pointed out as a main factor of educational achievement, and policy has turned previously informal and limited parental involvement into a mandate, aiming at generalizing it.

Interestingly, parental involvement is educational policy properly, that is, not just school policy, insofar as it articulates school and family as spaces of education. Nevertheless, in spite of its parent empowerment and democratic participation possibility, it represents a totalitarian movement in educational policy. First, it equates education with schooling. Second, by prescribing family education or aligning home education to the prevailing school curriculum, it penetrates the private realm and formalizes family educative practices. Because the obligation of parents to actively support academic learning is taken for granted, homework becomes a specific means of school (i.e., state) cultural imposition over the family and diverse ethnic groups. From this perspective, there is less space and time for other types of education, including informal and nonformal education related to various popular cultures.

Thus, educational policy enforcing parental involvement generalizes one model of family–school and school–community relations, consequently ignoring family and community social and cultural diversity. On the one hand, it assumes that it is the responsibility of the family to help with instruction and curricular goals because of the value it must place on education. On the other hand, if parental support is found wanting, it assigns as a task of the school and teachers to guide disadvantaged families or negligent parents, and to build or eventually transform the community (Cibulka & Kritek, 1996).

Historical and Cultural Background

The colonial era image of the common school initiated by parents who hired (then male) teachers in order to teach their children within rural communities seems to be the distant cultural origin of the current appeal to the family (Church & Sedlak, 1976; Guest & Tolnay, 1985; Kaestle, 1983). In contrast, at the end of the 19th century, when school became compulsory for children of urban industrial workers, mostly poor immigrants, a parallel movement of parent education emerged (Cravens, 1993; Grubb & Lazerson, 1982).

According to the puritan ethos that praises hard work, and to the liberal-meritocratic rhetoric that attributes socioeconomic success to school success, reinforced by the upward mobility of certain groups of immigrants who took advantage of educational and economic opportunities, the middle classes practiced a constant involvement with their children's education throughout the 20th century. The expansion of school enrollments at secondary and tertiary levels is seen as a result of the social mobility impetus (Labaree, 1997). However, when the critique of the social exclusion and school segregation of African-Americans, as well as the low performance of other minorities, emerged in the context of the 1960s civil rights movement, the educational solutions that followed (such as parent education within compensatory education programs) predominantly took the model of middle-class family–school relations as a norm.

In 1966, the renowned Coleman Report (Coleman, Campbell, Hobson, McPartland, Mood, Weinfeld, & York, 1966) stressed the importance of family background characteristics (the economic and educational resources of the home) for the differentiated school achievements of Native, Mexican, Puerto Rican, African, Asian, and White Americans, downplaying the weight of schools' physical and economic resources. At the same time in which it recognized that the sources of inequality of educational opportunities were "first in the home," it also pointed out "schools' ineffectiveness to free achievement from the impact of the home" (Coleman, 1966, p. 74).

Since then, educational research and policy have partly invested in "effective schools" (curricular and instructional reforms, teacher preparation, and professional development), but also in family child care and socialization processes that precede, support, or "cause" educational achievement, informing and legitimating educational interventions in the realm of the family in order to correct the "cultural deficit" and prevent the school failure of minority and disadvantaged groups.

Cultural deficit theory was strongly supported by research in cognitive psychology. According to Scott-Jones (1993), most of the literature on family influence on school achievement focused specifically on teaching strategies and language in the context of mother–child interactions: "American researchers concluded that the poor school achievement of low-income children was due to the impoverished language environment in their homes" (p. 247). Low-income mothers were less effective teachers than middle-class mothers due to such factors as "less praise, less asking questions, less orienting the child to the task, and more non-verbal communication" (p. 247).

The cultural deficit view of minority families and children led to a series of intervention programs, funded under Chapter 1 of the Elementary and Secondary Education Act, during the 1960s and 1970s. Head Start, for instance,

> ... provided not only parent-training activities but also a center-based educational component for preschool children and parent involvement in the governance of the program. Involvement in governance was intended to empower the low-income and minority parents who received Head Start services; in practice, however, Head Start came to concentrate on training parenting skills, as did other intervention programs. (Scott-Jones, 1993, p. 248)

The Contribution of Educational Research to Validate Parental Involvement

Legitimated by research in its importance and efficacy, parental involvement in schooling has been rhetorically constructed as both the problem and the solution for increasing school productivity and the academic performance of socially disadvantaged groups (Chavkin, 1993a, 1993b; Cibulka & Kritek, 1996; U.S. Department of Education, 1987; Henderson & Berla, 1994). As evidence of its importance as a research problem, since 1982, the American Educational Research Association (AERA) created a Special Interest Group named *Families as Educators*. Its mission is "to promote the study and dissemination of information on family social processes and home–school relationships that support children's education and development" —focusing, in short, on family education for school achievement (Families as Educators Special Interest Group, 1996, p. 1). According to Henderson and Berla (1994), "by 1987 . . . the subject had come into its own as a special topic of research. . . . Now, in 1994, the field has become a growth industry" (p. ix).

Henderson and Berla's (1994) report, *The Family is Crucial to Student Achievement*, published by the National Committee for Citizens in Education (NCCE) —whose mission is defined as "putting the public back in the public schools" (p. x) —provides a useful annotated bibliography of 66 titles (research reports, reviews, articles, and books), ranging from 1969 to 1993. Because they focused on family empowerment, student achievement, and effective schooling as a result of parental involvement, Henderson and Berla offered a particularly positive and conclusive reading of this research: "To those who ask whether involving parents will really make a difference, we can safely say that the case is closed" (p. x). In this context, Epstein (1996) expressed the present research agenda grounded on the concurrent implementation of partnership programs in the following terms: "We have moved from the question, Are families important for student success in school? to *If* families are important for children's development and school success, *how* can schools help all families conduct the activities that will benefit their children?" (p. 213).

An alternative critical reading of the research that supports parental involvement as valid policy may be offered as well, stressing the ideological basis of both interpretation of (necessarily limited) research findings and policy prescriptions drawn from them. I focus on three trends of research, based on Henderson and Berla's annotated bibliography: (a) evaluation of early intervention compensatory programs which incorporated a parental education component, including 33 studies of experimental and longitudinal design; (b) investigation of family background influence on student achievement, totaling 29 studies using both quantitative and qualitative approaches; and (c) critical studies of family–school cultural mismatch, represented by 4 titles only.

(a) The evaluation research that followed compensatory education programs basically intended to correlate increased parental (i.e., maternal) involvement with significant gains in academic achievement as measured by IQ and other academic performance tests (e.g., Goodson & Hess, 1975; Guinagh & Gordon, 1976; Irvine, 1979; Mowry, 1972; Olmsted & Rubin, 1982; Radin, 1972; cited in Henderson & Berla, 1994). Becher (1984, cited in Henderson & Berla, 1994), for instance, highlighted several key *family process variables* related to student achievement in elementary school: parents' high expectations for children, frequent interactions with them, modeling of learning and achievement, and actions as *teachers* of their children, using complex language and problem-solving strategies, and reinforcing what they learned in school. The policy rationale derived from this kind of research is that if "programs designed with extensive parental involvement can boost low income students' achievement to levels expected for middle-class students" (Henderson & Berla, 1994, p. 7), then parental involvement and training is a solution to inequity.

However, as pointed out by Lazar and Darlington (1978, cited in Henderson & Berla, 1994), parental involvement cannot be easily isolated and measured as a variable, though it is part of a cluster of factors considered necessary for program effectiveness. More recently, White, Taylor and Moss (1992, cited in Henderson & Berla, 1994) offered a comprehensive methodological critique, according to rigorous standards of reliability and validity, based on a review of 193 studies:

> Thus, it would be inappropriate to conclude, based on this data, that parent involvement in early intervention is not beneficial. Just as important, however, is the fact that no information exists in this admittedly indirect type of evidence to argue that parent involvement in early intervention will lead to any of the benefits that are often claimed. (p. 109)

Moreover, from a practical and dynamical point of view, experimental programs tend to create unique situations and, if successful, ideal models. Thus, there is no guarantee that the conditions and incentives fostered by a particular program, in a particular context, will be successfully reproduced elsewhere, let alone everywhere.

(b) Another significant trend of research focused on the influence of family processes (the home environment that encourages school learning) and family interactions with schools (mothers' active participation in school activities) on students' development, grades, test scores, high school graduation rates, and enrollment in higher education. The crucial point here is to establish "the extent to which family socioeconomic status (SES) determines the quality of student performance" (Henderson & Berla, 1994, p. 7). Some studies established the relative autonomy of educational and cultural factors (the role of parents' effort) in front of unfavorable socioeconomic conjunctures (e.g., Baker & Stevenson, 1986; Eagle, 1989; Kellaghan, Sloane, Alvarez, & Bloom, 1993; Stevenson & Baker, 1987; cited in Henderson & Berla, 1994), consequently suggesting that "family practices can have an effect independent of SES" (Henderson & Berla, 1994, p. 8). Other studies indicated that family practices (reading to children, guiding TV watching, and providing stimulating experiences) can be positively shaped by involvement with schools (e.g., Sattes, 1985; cited in Henderson & Berla, 1994), and that "the school can be a powerful force for building parent capacity and thereby buffer the negative consequences of low-income" (e.g., Cochran & Henderson, 1986; cited in Henderson & Berla, 1994, p. 46), thus altering the attitudes of powerless and excluded groups (e.g.,, Ziegler, 1987; cited in Henderson & Berla, 1994). Such research tends to corroborate an exaggerated belief in the power of individuals to overcome material limitations, as well as in the power of school policy to change home culture (where it is perceived as inadequate) in order to enhance school success and minimize educational inequalities.

The studies that focused specifically on families as learning environments basically compared parenting styles, strategies for teaching children at home, and expectations for academic performance associated with high-achieving and low-achieving students (e.g., Clark, 1983; Dornbusch, Ritter, Leiderman, Roberts, & Fraleigh, 1987; Scott-Jones, 1984, 1987; cited in Henderson & Berla, 1994). Their implicit premise is that families must provide the dispositions (Bourdieu & Passeron's *habitus*) toward school learning and success. Rumberger, Ghatak, Poulos, Ritter, and Dornbusch (1990, cited in Henderson & Berla, 1994), for instance, found that dropouts were more likely to have parents less involved in their education (specifically with homework and school events). In contrast, high achievers, across grade levels and social groups, were identified with the following home characteristics: daily routines for study, sleep, household chores, and limited TV watching; parent modeling of the values of learning, self-discipline, and hard work; parent expression of high but realistic expectations for achievement, and encouragement and reinforcement of school progress; reading, writing, and discussions among family members; and use of community resources, such as libraries. Other studies, however, pointed out that the parenting style associated with successful school performance is also associated with higher levels of income and education (e.g., Benson, Medrich, & Buckley, 1980; Eagle, 1989; cited in Henderson & Berla, 1994). Moreover, while particular forms of parent–child interactions and parent involvement at school may reduce the achievement deficit of low-SES children in elementary school, they *do not* overcome their disadvantages compared with their upper SES peers (Benson et al., 1980, cited in Henderson & Berla, 1994).

This line of research implicitly assumes the model of family related to school success: typically middle-class, affluent, usually with two parents and a full-time mother. Consequently, it prescribes a single family and parenting model, ignoring single parenthood, the increasing number of mothers who work long hours out of the home, the economic and health (including emotional) problems that affect many families, and the diversity of parenting styles related to material, cultural, and personal conditions. Another consequence is the endeavor to improve family environments and make them more educationally productive, prioritizing work habits over unproductive leisure activities (e.g., Clark, 1990; Kellaghan et al., 1993; cited in Henderson & Berla, 1994), instead of improving the quality of school and classroom learning. This tendency is evidenced by the titles of the following works: *Families as Educators: Time Use Contributions to School Achievement* (Benson et al., 1980, cited in Hendeson & Berla, 1994), and *Families as Partners in Educational Productivity* (Walberg, 1984, cited in Henderson & Berla, 1994). At a practical level, this view of families as educators originated formal *contracts*, sometimes including vouchers and stipends (e.g., Gillum, 1977, cited in Henderson & Berla, 1994), stipulating parents' tasks: to provide a special place in the home for study; to encourage the child daily through discussions; to attend to student's progress and compliment him/her on gains; and to cooperate with the teacher appropriately (e.g., Walberg, Bole, & Waxman, 1980, cited in Henderson & Berla, 1994).

(c) Few studies of family–school interactions have focused on class and cultural mismatch, referring to differences between values and ways of learning promoted at home and those promoted at school. Whereas the free time, money, cultural resources, and social networks of the middle class contribute to a productive match between home and school facilitating parents' interactions with teachers, working class culture promotes separation between home and school, limiting opportunities for collaboration and lowering teachers' expectations for students (Lareau, 1993; also Wong Fillmore, 1990, cited in Henderson & Berla, 1994). In addition, ethnic and language diversity create discontinuity between the types of socialization, child rearing, and skill development, natural in certain cultural groups, and the background or home preparation required of children in order to prosper in mainstream American public schools (Michaels, 1986; Wong Fillmore, 1990, cited in Henderson & Berla, 1994).

The cultural mismatch view and the knowledge about cultural diversity have moved educational interventions away from the cultural deprivation disabling approach to the direction of learning about and valuing the skills, strengths, and values of ethnic minority children and their families (e.g., Cummins, 1986, cited in Henderson & Berla, 1994). Wong Fillmore (1990, cited in Henderson & Berla, 1994), for instance, asserted that the more anchored children are in their primary culture, the greater their chances to adjust successfully to new environments. Consequently, policy derived from this view recommends increasing the overlap between home and school through programs that build on children's home experiences and help them learn how to apply cognitive and social skills learned at home to academic activities, while providing opportunities for them to acquire the strategies and outlooks expected in school (e.g., Kellaghan et al., 1993; Wong Fillmore, 1990; cited in Henderson & Berla, 1994). The challenge posed by this view, then, is to create effective schools that practice and teach cultural translation, contributing simultaneously to the conservation of cultural diversity and the transformation of school culture, while empowering students from the starting point of their particular cultures (Delpit, 1988; Heath, 1983).

The Current Policy Framework: Parental Involvement as a Resouce for School Sucess

Parental involvement in schooling has become the dominant paradigm of family–school relations in the U.S. As such, its political appeal seems to lie in its power to combine various social, economic, and cultural trends.

For example, in 1982, the Michigan State Board of Education issued a booklet entitled *Position Statement and Resource Guide on Involvement of Parents and Other Citizens in the Educational System*, recommending parental involvement in "*communicating* about schools, *training* to assist in school programs, and *marketing* the many positive aspects about school programs" (Michigan State Board of Education, 1982, Superintendent's Foreword). Recognizing "the value of active participation of citizenry in helping schools attain the educational goals identified by state and local communities," the "severe declines in resources" and "budget constraints," and survey results on the positive contribution of parents and other community members' involvement in schools, the document called upon parents' "services, interests, and commitment . . . to assist wherever practicable in all aspects of the school program" (pp. 1–2).

Indeed, the movement toward the family as a locus of education and school support has gained force under the conservative political tide of the 1980s, with the renewed pressures for excellence and a new quality education required for the productive sector, and the reactionary call for *family values* and *hard work* (Barton & Coley, 1992; National Commission on Excellence in Education, 1983). Since then, parental responsibility in education has been increasingly called on as a remedy for increasing school productivity, countering the failure of disadvantaged groups, and achieving both the individual's and the nation's economic success (Swap, 1993). Policy is justified on the grounds of "a growing body of research [that] suggests that increased family involvement is associated with higher mathematics and reading scores, decreased likelihood that a student will be suspended or expelled from school, and greater student participation in extracurricular school activities"

(National Education Goals Panel, 1995, p. 3; U.S. Department of Education, 1987). While the previous focus on "families as educators" referred to young children, current efforts at educational reform pose "the need to continue to engage families in the education of older children and adolescents" (Dornbusch & Ritter, 1988; Fehrmann, Keith, & Reimers, 1987; Jackson, 1989), suggesting this might be an antidote for school indiscipline and teen delinquency, and even school and family crises.

Furthermore, the policy and research agendas on family–school interactions have also adopted the current stress on cultural diversity, and again are targeting recent immigrants (Scott-Jones, 1993; Valdes, 1996). Programs like *Family Math* and *Family Science* (Programs for Educational Opportunity, 1995), for instance, have merged adult and child education, promising academic, social, and emotional gains for both students and parents.

On the other hand, progressive educators have also invested in parental empowerment as a strategy of educational reform within "a struggle to resuscitate the public sphere of public education" (Fine, 1993, p. 683). The promise of the partnership model is the implementation of a more productive family–school relation, resulting in family empowerment, school effectiveness, and success for all students. The formula goes like this: more parental involvement at home equates better school performance and longer attendance; and more parental involvement at school results in better schools. Especially optimistic, for it overlooks the culture wars (Hunter, 1991), is the hope to recover democratic values and practices by "allowing parents and citizens to participate in the governing of public institutions and to have the deciding voice in how children are to be educated" (Henderson & Berla, 1994, p. 19).

Finally, in 1994, the participation of parents in schools became the National Education Goal 8 under President Clinton's *Goals 2000: Educate America Act* (National Education Goals Panel, 1995). Thus, the *National Education Goals Report* states *Goal 8: Parental Participation*, and its related objectives, in terms of *family–school partnerships* that clearly assign parents a specific role in *academic* development:

> By the year 2000, every school will promote partnerships that will increase parental involvement and participation in promoting the social, emotional, and academic growth of children.

> Objectives:
> • Every State will develop policies to assist local schools and local educational agencies to establish programs for increasing partnership that respond to the varying needs of parents and the home, including parents of children who are disadvantaged or bilingual, or parents of children with disabilities.
> • Every school will actively engage parents and families in a partnership which supports the academic work of children at home and shared educational decision making at school.
> • Parents and families will help to ensure that schools are adequately supported and will hold schools and teachers to high standards of accountability. (National Education Goals Panel, 1995, p. 13)

Apparently (and rhetorically), partnerships should fulfill a variety of desirable (and supposedly compatible) needs: (a) of parents and the home, underscoring disadvantaged, bilingual, and disabled children; (b) of academic reinforcement at home; (c) of parental participation in educational decision making at school; (d) of adequate financial support of schools; and (e) of high standards of accountability for schools and teachers.

Family–school partnerships sound right. Initiatives are under way, and the National Association of Parents and Teachers recently published *National Standards for Parent/Family Involvement Programs* (National PTA, 1997). However, what are the meanings and implications of assigning parents a specific responsibility for the *academic* growth of their children?

Homework seems to be the least visible aspect of this policy. The object of specific, explicit, and detailed policy at district and school building levels (Cooper, 1994; Roderique, Polloway,, Cumblad, Epstein & Bursuck, 1994), since the 1980s (before the formalization of parental involvement as national policy), homework had already silently penetrated homes, and impacted everyday family life. In effect, homework policies have redefined "*the home as an extension of the classroom*" and homework "as an assignment to be completed outside of school hours *preferably at home*," thus avoiding extended school hours or other community alternatives. While one of the declared functions of homework is to "keep parents informed and involved in their child's learning," there are "*consequences for not completing homework*," which explicitly include student after-school *detention* (East Lansing Educational Foundation, 1996, p. 14, italics added).

Furthermore, homework has become an integral part of the evaluation of learning, ranging from 40% to 60% of term grades (especially in middle but also in high school), even when it is graded based only on punctuality and completion. New homework formats have appeared, such as *interactive homework*, with sections for parents to work with the students (for instance, using math and science while preparing dinner), comment, and sign (Epstein, 1994; Gallagher, 1994; Mafnas, Flis-Calvo, & Dionio, 1993; Olympia, Sheridan, & Jenson, 1994; Orman, 1993; Wisdom, 1993). From the school perspective, the desirable picture of the family is that of parents and students discussing homework around the dinner table.

It is important to note that participation in school governance is unlikely and unworkable for parents as a group, but absence of participation does not imply direct and immediate costs for children. In contrast, and despite its unfeasibility, parents' participation in the home becomes practically compulsory, due to the evident sanctions imposed by homework.

THE PROBLEM

The educational policy focus on families, previously illustrated, carries implications that deserve careful examination:

- It denies the specificity of schooling within modern education, blurring the distinction between formal and informal education.

. • It overlooks the professional status of teachers, ignoring their special knowledge and preparation, by suggesting that the parent can play the teacher at home.

• It is based on a single family model: affluent, with a full-time wife and mother (Thorne & Yalom, 1992), and on the myth of the self-reliant U.S. family (Coontz, 1992), in a time of increasing economic struggle, maternal employment, single-parent families, and family stress.

• It assigns parents the obligation of providing for *academic*, as well as social and emotional, growth of children, overlooking family differences in economic, social, and cultural forms of capital that are converted in school advantage or disadvantage (Bourdieu, 1987).

• It imposes on parents the conception that the home should be a setting for the explicit and intentional development of the school curriculum, and the obligation to convert family activities into an extension of class activities, in detriment of cultural pluralism, as well as family leisure and rest.

• It promises to "respond to the varying needs of parents and the home" (National Education Goals Panel, 1995, p. 13) instead of the educational, specifically academic, needs of children, adopting, at least rhetorically, a social assistance model of schooling,

• It implies the reeducation of the parents as a precondition for the education of children, amplifying the scope of obligation of the school.

• It suggests that schools and families have equal power in deciding the education that is carried at school, seducing parents with the possibility of participating in educational decision making at school, which demands time, knowledge, and collective power.

• It attributes to parents, though vaguely, formal, direct, and enhanced responsibility in *ensuring* support for the public school.

• It assigns parents the role of inspectors of schools' and teachers' accountability, inciting latent conflicts and eventually setting parents against teachers.

• It attributes to varying and diverse families the establishment of high (and common!) educational standards, moreover omitting currently conflictive issues of content and values.

• It diverts the focus of educational improvement from the classroom to the home.

Policies of parental involvement and family–school partnership, as just formulated, seem to be grounded on ambiguous conceptions that schools can change families and at the same time *depend* on families for change and improvement, and that families are deficient and at the same time have an important role in responding to the school's agenda and/or charging school's accountability, while prescribing (through moral rhetoric) and adopting (through teachers' expectations) a total approach to family educational accountability.

The present call for more family accountability in education reduces education (a broad social phenomenon carried by various institutions and cultural practices) to schooling, confuses parenting with teaching, and limits schooling to economic purposes and outcomes. The intriguing fact is that precisely when schools have extended their functions in order to encompass affective, social, and moral development objectives, and assumed "shared parenting" (Elkind, 1995; Sedlak & Schlossman, 1985), they have come to charge families specifically with academic support. Furthermore, the intrusion into the educative practices of families (by requiring specific forms of academic support and assigning more homework) represents an attempt at making the *home curricula* uniform, at a time when diversity is celebrated in the school curriculum.

Significance

There are at least three important issues underlying the problem of family–school educational responsibilities.

The first is *equity*. To the extent that families are culturally different and dispose of unequal cultural resources in aligning with school cultural norms, policy that stimulates family input or parental participation in school will enhance differentiated educational outcomes.

On the one hand, current policy discourse claims the general desirability and effectiveness of parental involvement in schooling. On the other hand, though this is not explicit, it is likely that policy actions will target those families *at risk* and those parents *in need* of parental reeducation, trying to compensate for disadvantages. Unfortunately, the reach of educational policy is limited by more powerful socioeconomic factors, and families at risk are generally the least likely to take advantage and benefit from educational opportunities in the first place. Thus, there is a chance that even compensatory policy efforts will simply feed on the existent vicious cycle: low socioeconomic conditions and low educational achievement.

The second issue is the *emotionally charged and conflictive character of family–school relations* regarding personal and collective interests, and the ambivalence of the teaching role within the division of educational work between family and school and the specific function of social differentiation performed by the educational system.

—— Long ago, Waller (1965) defined parents and teachers as "natural enemies," proposing a conflict of private and public interests, in which parents are more concerned with the individual characteristics and needs of their children than teachers can possibly be in the context of mass public schooling. Parents depend on schools and teachers for educating their children (as school provides for the main, legitimate, and compulsory occupation of youngsters) and on the ethics of personal and social success within and via school. Therefore, they are concerned that their children might be subject to injustice and harm.

Teachers are committed to benefiting all children, but their role includes evaluating students differentially. Hence, attributing the lacks of students to family background excuses teachers' performance and its effect on students' learning, thereby enhancing parents' vulnerability in turn, as parents tend to feel deeply affected by their children's failures. But teachers are also vulnerable in that they are concerned with their professional standing in front of parental interference and negative evaluation (and its eventual repercussions on the institutional evaluation of their professional performance). Thus, there is a perennial dispute of accountability in student performance in school, most evident in student failure: Did the school and teacher fail to offer conditions of learning or did the student continuously lack family support and could not take advantage of what the school offered?

The third issue is a nuance of the previous and a perverse effect of the current bent of public education toward family accountability: *the ideological, emotional, and moral charge over families.* As already mentioned, a significant trend of the educational literature and a quite common posture among teachers is that it is natural and desirable that families (parents) do the school curriculum at home, according to the school and teachers' requests. The advocates of active parental participation in children's schooling do not consider the possibility that some parents may be unable or even unwilling to participate. In this context, parental *choice* not to participate tends to be seen negatively as *omission* or *negligence* by the school.

The fact that parental participation is taken for granted as a natural behavior, or assumed and expected by the school as necessarily consensual and positive, suggests that efforts should be made at promoting it when it is found lacking. Neither implications for families nor for schools and teachers are considered. Even when participation is positively envisioned as opportunity for individual empowerment (of parents) and as a medium of institutional transformation (of schools), the price it charges both individuals and institutions is overlooked.

In general, the rhetoric of parental involvement ranges from a more individual to a more social perspective, but it still places the burden on the family in terms of improving student achievement and/or schools. According to a more individual, consumer's choice perspective, parents should learn how to exercise parental responsibility in terms of control of their children's education (Berger, 1985), and how to develop a customized relationship with their children's school. According to a more social perspective, parents should participate in order to reconstruct and improve particular schools and the public education system. However, both perspectives seem to ignore the consequences of the play of cultural capital in enhancing the social advantages of a few and the very limits of many (working-class, cultural minority, single-parent) families regarding social participation.

Moreover, the ideologies of family choice, parental involvement, and family–school partnership bear a nostalgic trace of the original community school, and the contradictory assumption that families have the power to transform school as a social institution, and that schools depend principally and directly on families for change or for success. The very diversity and various difficulties of the family as a social institution nowadays are simply omitted.

If educators and policymakers are concerned with equity, with the role of families in producing differentiated school outcomes, and particularly with the effects that ideological and moral pressures on families may have over children, and are willing to productively manage and minimize conflicts and emotional distress among students, parents and teachers, they should attend to such issues.

ANALYTICAL APPROACH

This book focuses on the articulations and implications of family–school relations as an object of educational policy. Understanding policy as both discourse and practice, I explore current concepts, approaches, and problems of parental involvement in schooling, as framed by policy proposals, grounded by theoretical and empirical literature, and reflected in my own experience as a parent and educator. Thus, I inquire into a variety of literary and experiential sources about the roles of school, family, and educational policy, and related background issues of educational accountability, the public character of school, and equity.

In order to explicate my analytical approach, I next spell out my assumptions about family–school relations and educational policy, and the specific questions, background issues, and kinds of evidence and sources guiding the inquiry and informing further analysis.

Conceptual framework

Schools and families, as social institutions, are interrelated and interdependent, but also relatively autonomous, as they are situated in distinct spaces and times, respond to diverse needs of daily life, and carry specific practices toward distinct goals, while eventually pursuing common goals. They represent contingent and variable historical arrangements, and are singly differentiated in terms of conditions, workings, and commitments, despite general structures and functions. Moreover, they work within a larger social system, represented by the state. Thus, as school and family are inserted in and affected by larger socioeconomic and political arrangements, their relative power in determining individual chances is variable and uncertain.

Relationships between schools and families are complex, multiangled, and affected by both family diverse and evolving concrete social circumstances, and changing educational policies and practices. On the one hand, the reach of school policy onto the family is necessarily limited and uneven, as it is the power of the family to influence school outcomes. On the other hand, while families and children are generally vulnerable within social dynamics, schools are especially powerful mechanisms of social exclusion (Bourdieu & Passeron, 1977; Lamont & Lareau, 1988). However, a certain cultural continuity between certain types of families and schools enhances the possibilities of their mutual influence and alignment (Bourdieu & Passeron, 1977; Lareau, 1993).

Family and school educational responsibilities have evolved historically in the direction of increasing extension and specialization of the school role. However, the dynamic articulations between these institutions still need to be conceptualized within specific settings, circumstances, and practices. Bourdieu and Passeron's (1977) concept of *cultural capital*, within a theory of social reproduction via the legitimization of certain forms of symbolic power, exchanges, and conversions, illuminated those articulations by focusing specifically on the role of the educational system in linking individual behaviors, cultural resources, social class, formal and informal practices, and institutional standards.

Bourdieu and Passeron (1977) defined cultural capital as:

> ... the cultural goods transmitted by the different family pedagogic actions, whose value qua cultural capital varies with the distance between the cultural arbitrary imposed by the dominant pedagogic action and the cultural arbitrary inculcated by the family pedagogic action within the different groups or classes. (p. 30)

In explaining the role of education in class reproduction within a cultural framework, Bourdieu (1977) posed the natural alignment of middle and upper class families with school and academic culture, and the subordination of low class families within school and high culture. In other words, the school's curriculum and standards (both formal and informal) represent the dominant culture and implicitly capitalize on the differentiated cultural resources of families and individuals (the *habitus* or dispositions acquired in the process of primary socialization), inflating or deflating them, while proclaiming neutrality. Individuals, families, and classes dispose unevenly of the kind of cultural capital necessary to invest in acquiring educational and social success.

The path to educational equity, as suggested by Bourdieu and Passeron's framework, depends on educational policies and practices assuming *explicitly* that the school adopts the dominant culture, and that many students lack the required cultural resources to succeed in it. Consequently, educational policies and practices should *neutralize*, as much as possible, what Lareau (1993) calls "home advantage," while offering compensatory resources and opportunities—for instance, teaching disadvantaged students what Delpit (1988) calls "the language of power." Along this line, educational policy should focus on maximizing the role of school resources while minimizing the impact of family resources on learning and achievement in the interest of social justice.

I realize that the possibility of the educational system playing the role described earlier depends on its both acknowledging and exercising its relative autonomy (making its proper political action explicit) in front of the broader socioeconomic system, which in turn depends on political circumstances. While the role of the educational system is ultimately social reproduction (in the broad sense of cultural conservation), social reproduction is not automatic but a complexly mediated process, which allows for certain choices in the direction of more or less equity.

Parental involvement represents a specific choice in educational policy. In the best hypothesis, granted its viability, it extends compensatory education to the family realm. In the worst hypothesis, by regulating the educational contribution of families, it homogenizes family culture, and legitimizes parental evaluation by the school. Along this line, two questions stand out: Is parental involvement—as a strategy to enhance academic learning and outcomes—a legitimate and effective policy? And, is parental participation in school conducive to more equity?

Policy rhetoric generally and continually affirms a commitment to improving learning for all students. Parental involvement, the case in point, is proposed as a measure of general benefit: "Schools must inform and involve all families, including those with different cultural backgrounds, to gain their ideas and assistance in helping all children succeed in school" (Epstein, 1993, p. ix). However, such a general directive bears implications.

On the one hand, educational policy sets one agenda for all families—specifically about how families can contribute to the curricular goals and their children's school success—disregarding prior diversity of class and culture, the differentiated cultural capital which is the currency of school success (Bourdieu, 1977). In this way, educational policy subordinates families to schools by clearly setting the educational agenda and assigning parents the job of teacher-aide.

But, on the other hand, families have different life conditions and arrangements, and various views and feelings about life, education, and educational responsibility. They respond differently to school expectations and policy mandates on schooling depending on material and cultural circumstances, social class, and individual behaviors and values (Lareau, 1993). Therefore, families do not necessarily benefit from *opportunities* to participate and exert influence on their children's education, either in school (such as attending parent–teacher conferences, discussing the school curriculum) or at home (tutoring homework). Moreover, most families are in a position of lesser power to influence school policies and practices and to take advantage of educational opportunities for their children. The visible exception consists of upper middle-class families, which have *privatized* the public school (Lareau, 1993), and set the model for all families (Berger, 1985).

If and when policy efforts fail to benefit all families and students, they undoubtedly harm some of them. This is an effect of the contradictory character of policies that define the common good in terms that generalize the desirability of a limited situation or practice (such as parental participation as an efficient mediator of school success), without providing the effective means (which are ultimately beyond their reach) to make that possibility viable for those who do not fit in it but *should* aim at reaching it.

Thus, before prescribing parental participation and implementing mechanisms to enhance parental involvement in schooling, educational policy should attend to important underlying questions: Does the nominally democratic state effectively represent the interests of all families in the realm of public schooling and how can it best represent? Can all families and children equitably benefit from schooling as it is and how could they best benefit? More specifically: Is it possible and reasonable to turn all families (or certain *ignorant* or *ill-equipped* families) into efficient mediators of their children's school success? Furthermore: Is it desirable and possible from the points of view of these diverse families to actively invest in their children's school performance? Such questions should precede and continuously ground policy goals, designs, implementation plans, and practical decisions within the school and the classroom.

While I acknowledge the need to develop a theoretical framework for analyzing family–school relationships and their mutual implications, I am aware of the enormity of such a task. My simple claim is that educators need to envision a theoretical picture if they are concerned with the broad and subtle implications of their practices. I solely hope to offer an interpretation of the articulation of theoretical and empirical elements in educational policy, pointing out the contradictory role of liberal educational policy (the discourse of opportunity), particularly when it explicitly aims at reaching the family, in building structures and enforcing practices for the play of cultural capital in the process of social reproduction via education.

Questions for Inquiry

What are the rationales behind present policy efforts aiming at connecting family and school? How are the need and benefits of a close family–school partnership characterized? Is the aim to empower the family—granting families more control over schools and choice over instructional contents and practices? Is the aim to make schooling more effective—subordinating families to the school agenda, and elevating academic learning at the expense of private choices? How are the specific educational roles of each institution depicted within the family–school partnership? What expectations and demands are posed to the family and what implications do they create? How is the idea of a public school redefined within the partnership model? What is the role of educational policy toward the family? What would a close rhetorical reading of the policy and academic literature on the subject say about these issues?

My core analytical issue is the role and implications of parental involvement in school within the articulation of school and family by educational policy. However, this issue is intertwined with important background and parallel issues: (a) the power, both individual and institutional, to define and benefit from education and schooling; (b) the reach and viability of public policy, especially in relation to the private space and practices; (c) the meaning of a public school, including purposes, knowledge, conditions of learning, standards of assessment, the definition of the kind of education that can benefit all (diverse) families, and the delimitation of parental influence and choice within its curriculum and organization; (d) equity, conceived strategically not only as equal opportunities to learn within equal school conditions, but as positive discrimination (extra and special opportunities) to compensate for unequal (previous and external) social conditions; (e) and the division of work and educational accountability between teachers and parents, including the definition of teacher professionalism.

The issues just stated suggest interesting questions: To what extent are family education and schooling equivalent? Who defines education and school success? Who contributes to and who benefits from education and schooling? On what forms and kinds of contribution is school success dependent? Who does the educational work, and who is accountable for school success? To what extent are all families and parents able to contribute to school success? Should families be entitled or compelled to contribute to schooling by means of direct work? How is teacher professionalism affected by parental participation in instruction? What are the legitimacy, viability, and efficacy of the educational policy reach over families? To what extent can policy induce or regulate families' educational efforts—for instance, change roles, practices and values, or enhance certain practices of certain families? To what extent should public school depend on families and parents playing a particular role? What is the legitimate and viable range of parental involvement and choice within the context of a public school?

I certainly do not answer each one of these questions in this volume. In posing them, however, my aim is twofold. First, they illustrate the complexity of the focus on parental involvement as a strategy for enhancing school outcomes by pointing out implicit relations and implications, and some of its problematic aspects, such as the beliefs in a *natural* partnership between school and family, based on cultural continuity and functional affinity, and in the general benefit of the policy's reach over families. Second, they create a necessary context of discussion: Definitions or redefinitions of the specific educational roles of schools and families imply a reconceptualization of public education, and the question of to what extent families should be accountable for school success, and why, refers to the limits and possibilities of equity within educational policy rationales.

Data and Sources

In this book I mainly explore discourses: educational policy proposals regarding family–school relations, implicit or explicit theoretical formulations on the role of the family in schooling, and exemplars of empirical research that provide evidence of problems affecting those relations and justification for policy solutions aiming at improving them.

I understand discourses as both representations of practices (critiques and justifications of actual or desirable practices), and as (relatively) autonomous practices in their own right. Moreover, I consider the connection between policy and research (the translation of empirically based explanations into proposals of intervention and strategies for action) as a discursive practice subject to various interpretations. I also assume that interpretation, by individuals and groups (professionals) with particular motivations and beliefs, antecedes the very conceptualization of research and production of empirical evidence. Finally, it is important to remember that policy has influenced research and that research has its own politics.

The recent call on families and parents as educators, and policy rationales for family–school collaboration bear two dimensions: one relative to what is happening (an empirical-interpretive aspect), and another relative to what is aimed at (an ideological-normative aspect). Both dimensions—the definitions of problems and solutions that inform policy proposals (discourse) and implementation (practice)—are rhetorical.

Therefore, my data are various forms of discourse, mainly written texts (research findings, policy rationales, and other pertinent education literature), but also reflection on personal experiences. Because family–school relations as an object of educational policy encompass various angles and issues, my analysis draws on a variety of sources: selected theoretical and empirical academic literature, basically historical and sociological, policy documents, school newsletters, newspapers, and eventually anecdotes. A few salient pieces deserve a closer focus: Bourdieu and Passeron's (1977) theory of cultural and social reproduction via education; Coleman's (1966, 1967, 1987) discussion of the roles of families and schools in American education; and Lareau's (1993) empirical findings on the mediation of social class or socioeconomic status in shaping parental expectations and actions toward school and teachers, and teachers' requirements and responses to students and parents.

In reading the research-based policy recommendations regarding the role of families in student achievement and the specific actions of teachers and parents, I found myself rather skeptical about its accuracy and prospect. The sources of my skepticism were my own experiences and learning in relation to schools, along my life course: first, as a child and a student within my own family and social group in Brazil; later, as a parent dealing with private schools, and as a teacher educator dealing with public schools, also in Brazil; and, more recently, as a parent handling U.S. public schools. Reflecting on such personal experiences provided both temporal and spatial perspective, and motivation to inquire further.

While my empirical evidence is experiential and second-hand, my primary data are arguments. Regarding the normative aspect of policy, I question the explicit and implicit assumptions that guide definitions of problems, proposed actions, and expected outcomes, and discuss their implications in the light of the available theoretical, and empirical elements. Specifically, in mapping this rhetorical terrain, I consider how the available empirical findings and knowledge claims on the role of families in school success support certain policy choices, and whether the proposed solutions appear consistent with theoretical elements or, else, contradictory. In addition, as a window into the intricacies of the family–school educational partnership, I provide an analysis of homework as a practice of transferring schoolwork to the home, and its various meanings (as a policy, curricular conception, and instructional practice) and implications for teachers and parents.

Based on such exploratory analysis, I hope to draw and contribute to a broad—precarious, but indispensable—framework for analyzing the complex relationships between families and schools and the role of educational policy in articulating them.

2

Family–School Interactions: Lessons From Personal Experience

My personal interest in family–school relations derives in great part from my own experience as a parent relating to my children's school. I am also a teacher educator and I have frequently heard how teachers refer to families and parents when they talk about students, specifically how they tend to attribute the difficulties they experience with students to the family environment and lack of parental support. Finally, I am a foreigner trying to make sense of diverse cultures, presently in the United States, and previously in Brazil. Over time, I have faced episodes and collected anecdotes across a variety of contexts that have sustained my perception of the problematic relations between families and schools.

In this chapter, I offer an idiosyncratic account and reflection on my own involvement with the problem, as a child within my family and the schools I attended, as a mother (and also a single parent) in front of my children's schools, and as an educator with a special interest in the public school system. Reviewing this personal context substantiated my initial impulse to study the issue, and making it explicit provided a preliminary opportunity for inquiry.

DISCOVERING THE PROBLEM

I first realized the existence of a family–school problem when I did a brief exploratory study in poor urban and rural elementary schools, in João Pessoa, Brazil, in 1981 (de Carvalho & Ramalho, 1983). In exploring factors of low student achievement through interviews with principals, teachers, and mothers, an interesting (apparently unrelated) problem emerged: a mutual dissatisfaction and distrust between school and family, more openly expressed by the teachers than by the mothers, and especially evident in the rural context. Generally, mothers expressed the expectation that students should learn in school and that teachers should take a positive interest in their children. However, those mothers seemed defensive toward school. As the interviewers were associated with the school, rural mothers spoke little and carefully, while urban mothers (in whose discourse education appeared as a positive value and a condition for upward social mobility) promptly (and strategically) avowed that they liked the school and the teacher.

Family–school relations are usually taken for granted because it is believed that schools serve families and that families need and benefit from schools. I was quite astonished then, as I approached a rural home with my colleague, two strangers that we were, when I heard a boy announce to his mother: "Mom, here comes the school police."

Parental Involvement in Preschool

During that time, my first child was starting his school life in a private, alternative, *maternal school*, a common name for kindergartens in Brazil. Maternal schools are usually small, specialized preschools, or branches of larger primary and secondary schools, not day-care centers, and serve children from 2 to 6 years old. *Alternative* schools are the progressive ones, set in more natural environments (big yards, trees, gardens, and sometimes animals), with a great deal of outdoor activities (thanks to the warm climate), and with children playing in the sand and water, moving freely around, all day. Pedagogically, alternative schools offer sophisticated developmental programs based on Piaget, Montessori, Freinet, ecological, sensory, *free-arts* frameworks, psychoanalytical approaches, Vygotskyan constructivism, and anything else novel, scientific, liberating, and appealing. These schools explicitly distinguish themselves from the traditional kindergartens, which are criticized for doing a combination of naïve, spontaneous play, and mechanical preparation for literacy by mimicking elementary school activities that put pressure on children.

In those alternative schools, and at this age level, parental involvement was very intense and complicated. So it was that I watched a few *school splits*. This was an interesting phenomenon: High-educated parents, teachers, psychologists, and school administrators, who had (or developed, despite apparent cultural homogeneity) different philosophical, psychological, and pedagogical commitments, expressed strong disagreements in the parents' meetings over nuances of the pedagogical practice and values conveyed by the curriculum. There were cases of some parents' stronger influence on the school curriculum and administration, which aroused rivalry among the parents. Cases of school interference in family routines caused further conflicts. After a time, groups polarized and it became impossible to compromise. As a result, one of the groups (of parents, teachers, and owners) left the school and started a new school with an alternative theoretical and practical approach.

I attribute the intensity of middle-class parental involvement in private preschool in Brazil to the early age of students and to a central concern with their emotional well-being. Middle-class parents who *have to* send their very young children to school (a new phenomenon due to women's increasing participation in the labor market and/or lack of domestic help) feel ambiguous and insecure about throwing them into the unknown, larger world, and into relationships with strangers, and thus inspect the school environment as much as they can. Participation might alleviate their anxiety and uncertainty over the values and practices—especially the affective climate—their children will encounter in school. Therefore, it is understandable that they project their views onto the school and try to influence it accordingly. In this context, relationships in Brazilian (at least middle-class) preschools mimic the family by displaying much physical contact and gestures of affection. Caretakers and teachers (also in public elementary schools) are even called *aunts*.

There are two striking aspects in this recent alternative private school movement. First, there is the fact that homogeneous, middle- and upper middle-class, highly educated parents do not succeed in compromising over a common educational project. Second, the occurrence of a split reduces the size of a school whenever it grows too fast. In fact, forms and intensity of parental involvement appear to be associated with school size, which facilitates or restrains direct, open, and collective participation. As I noticed from experience, parents' active participation in school as a *collective dynamic* constitutes a complicated issue in its own right, involving scale, parents' resources and values, school organizational features, openness of school personnel, and ideological affinities among parents and school personnel.

Family Distance From Public Schools

In Brazil, the kind of parental involvement in alternative private preschools, as just described, in which parents fight for influence and control, contrasts with the family–school relations prevalent in most public schools and traditional religious or secular private primary and secondary schools, which are usually larger and more rigidly structured. This other kind of school–family relation is one of distance and exclusive school control over the pedagogic process.

For one thing, as children grow older and more independent, parental involvement naturally tends to decrease. But school in Brazil is generally seen as a world apart from home, clearly public and ruled by its own edicts, probably due to a history of late supply of public education services and operational autonomy relative to families and communities. Thus, parental participation in the definition of the educational service has never been a cultural tradition in the public school. In private schools, parents tend to act as interested *consumers* in various degrees and forms, and consequently school control against parental interference assumes an ambiguous and subtle character. Interestingly, whereas school personnel in public schools might ignore families because they have job security, administrators and teachers in private schools *see* the direct relation between their earnings and students' fees, assuming a position of deference toward families while holding control.

Since the expansion of Brazilian public schooling in the 1960s, laments over family disinterest (basically referring to lack of home preparation) have been commonly heard and presented as one of the explanations for the high rates of school failure of poor children. The rhetoric of blaming the family has been an extension of the rhetoric of blaming the victim (i.e., the child), persisting as a defense against the rhetoric of blaming the teacher, the main person responsible for instruction and its outcomes. Thus, teachers constantly refer to certain families' lack of cooperation regarding specific problems and particular students, and parents' absence at school meetings, despite two widely recognized facts: (a) poor parents are under-schooled or illiterate; and (b) when attending school meetings, parents mostly hear teachers' complaints about their children's learning difficulties and/or lack of discipline. However, public school teachers officially are not supposed to expect much from socioeconomically burdened families in Brazil.

Of course Brazilian progressive educators have hoped that parents' contribution to education, as genuine political-democratic participation, would appropriately flourish in the context of the public school. But despite policy efforts to establish a model of public governance of schools through parent–teacher associations, parent representatives in school councils, and municipal and state councils of education, little has been accomplished in terms of parental participation in the public school system. On the one hand, poor and working-class parents (who comprise the majority of the population) have kept away from school, for obvious reasons. On the other hand, the retreat of the middle class from the public school continues to be lamented, as this group's level of expectations and demands is seen as an important condition to improve the quality of public education.

Parents as Consumers in Private Schools

Since educational reforms of the 1970s, the Brazilian middle class has been increasingly shifting their children to private schools, because of the so-called *decadence* of public school, the result of its cheap expansion, *de-elitization*, and loss of quality. A new kind of private school has emerged locally (and some have spread nationally, through franchises) as a clear commercial enterprise, basically committed to profit. These new educational enterprises contrast flagrantly with the formerly dominant religious private schools, based on an ethics of community service and affinity with families.

Middle-class parents have an ambiguous relationship with such new private schools (as indicated by the fact that their owners are called *sharks*), and deplore the merchandizing of education. The parents certainly take advantage of the competition among the schools, but are also suspicious that schools will fake their own advertised offers, as well as parents' demands. Moreover, parents are aware of their own limits as demanding consumers, for it would be disastrous to move children to a new school whenever they find reason for dissatisfaction and do not have their complaints settled.

During the 1980s, due to high rates of inflation, private school consumers exerted tight control over school fees, demanding both regulation from the government, *transparent* budgets and *reasonable* levels of profit from each private school administration. Yet, the very fact that parents choose and buy the best quality education they can afford (and eventually battle over its price) limits their participation in the process (and content) of education.

Parents as Producers in Cooperative Schools

Although some middle-class educators have lived the contradiction of defending the public schools and sending their kids to private schools, while continuing to idealize the role of parental participation in public schools, other pragmatic developments have been going on in Brazil. As a reaction to the high cost and unsatisfactory quality of private schools, some parents have started a new polemic movement of *cooperative schools*, in which a public school (generally a well-located and conserved building) is governed by a parent association, through an executive committee of volunteers, and may charge direct financial contributions from parents—a monthly payment, just like a private school.

This initiative has been the object of ideological debates over whose responsibility it is to provide for good quality education (some arguing that it is the state's) and over the implications of direct financial contributions from parents (some pointing out that it promotes differentiation among public schools). There have been conflicts between teachers and parents within the cooperative school management, as teachers felt subordinated to parents. There have also been conflicts among teachers from cooperative and other public schools, involving the teacher's union, due to parents' attempts to increase the salaries of cooperative school teachers, thus threatening the principle of equal pay for public school teachers. In summary, critics of the cooperative school have denounced the *privatization of the public school* by some middle-class parents who have returned to the public school, but continue investing in their own interests at the level of one particular school.

Such situations show that parental conceptions of educational obligation, choices, and possibilities of participation in schooling are limited, complicated, and, moreover, dependent on concrete needs and resources related to social class. Thus, participation aiming at influencing the quality of education requires substantial investment of time, effort, and knowledge, implying a direct role in the production of the service—a choice only available to some interested upper and middle-class parents. And yet, access to high quality education—exempt of any form of active participation—has always been possible for those who can buy exclusive, tailored, and expensive educational services.

Interestingly, parents who participate (with time and effort) in their children's formal education have done it primarily at home through the institution of homework, a somewhat obscure form of partnership.

Homework and Middle-Class Mothers

As a child growing up in Brazil in the 1960s, I frequented a half-day school (a period of 4 hours), which still remains the norm today, for economic reasons. I spent the morning hours at home doing homework with my brothers around the dinner table, and was not allowed to play before getting it done. My mother made sure we complied with the schoolwork, but she herself did not take interest or enjoy getting involved with it. She had a degree in law, an unusual career for women then, and had given up work to be a mother and housewife, but seemed frustrated with her domestic role.

I knew other mothers in the neighborhood who took as their daily task to supervise their children's homework and reinforce the school program. Those were full-time mothers with university degrees, who saw it as natural to perform an academic role at home. Their method was to check closely what had been taught the previous school day, and what their children had or had not learned well, in order to drill it. They routinely performed oral question and answer exercises, giving immediate feedback, and tested their children's learning before they left for school.

Different from my mother's generation, I had my children when I was a full-time professional. It was very disturbing for me to leave my first child at preschool when he was just 12 months old. It was hard to work, find good baby-sitters to take care of him at home the rest of the day, and get good quality time with him. Yet, soon I had two more children.

By the time my oldest child finished elementary school, I decided to transfer the three from the alternative Montessorian school they had frequented to a *traditional* school. I had no doubt they were very happy in that school, but I found that the oldest had not learned as much as I expected at the end of elementary school. I judged, not without concern, that it was time for them to experience massive dull teaching, to frequent an old building with thick walls, and thus I chose a high-standard Marist (Catholic) school. My problems with homework began then.

In the Montessorian school, my children never brought schoolwork home, and so they were unaccustomed to doing homework. I would leave work by 11:30 a.m. on a 2-hour break, in order to eat lunch with them, check their homework, and drive them to school, just to find out that they had spent the morning playing and watching TV. So, I had to hire a private tutor to sit with them every morning and help them do their homework *independently*, a goal she never accomplished, as she became totally indispensable in my family life.

Parents Versus Experts

As I attended the regular parents' meetings in the traditional religious school, I noted a rhetoric of subtly pointing at families' lacks and all the *extras* that the school environment and its professionals provided. I noticed an emphasis on the psychological needs of children and teenagers and the friendliness and involvement of teachers who were constantly listening to the students' *family* problems, especially teenagers who didn't have anyone to talk at *home*. Given that, I wondered whether they had any time left to teach the academic curriculum! I also felt that the school professionals (principals, pedagogic coordinators, teachers, and psychologists) talked to the parents in a peculiar style, as if they were talking to children.

Once I was called to a specific meeting with one of the school psychologists, because my fourth-grade son had disrupted class. After informing me that my son and another boy were caught throwing little pieces of paper containing obscene drawings, she immediately started an interview with me about sexual education in my family. As I perceived her professional attempt to find a problem in my home, I counteracted by pointing out that whereas in my house there were no pornographic materials, the school lavatory walls were decorated with obscene graffiti. I told her I felt that my son was a normal child, and suggested that "he certainly had learned that in school." As for the inappropriate class behavior, I thought the school should deal directly with the student and apply its disciplinary norms instead of calling me.

The school psychologist explained that they normally called parents in order to avoid further complaints. I expressed my view: I thought it unsound to expect that parents could prevent children's misbehavior in school, and I believed that problems created in the school environment, resulting from its particular patterns of organization, actions, or omissions, should be solved by the school professionals, according to their best wisdom. I also suggested that she could make better use of her time by intervening in the school setting and dealing directly with the problems generated there than by calling parents to inquire about their family life, in order to explain a child's behavior in a particular circumstance. If the school did not feel quite sure about the best disciplinary practices, and wanted to find out about parents' views and values, a survey would be a good start.

But surveys or other straightforward approaches to all parents were never tried while my children attended that school. This episode reinforced my perception that an attitude of focusing on individual cases constructed as problematic, and of problematizing the family, is part of the school culture and practices, just as I had found to be the case in the discourse of public school teachers elsewhere (de Carvalho, 1989). I view this attitude as detrimental in lieu of focusing on the school and improving its practices. It is doubtful that educators, counselors, and psychologists have already studied and solved the problems generated in the school context so well, that they are willing to extend their expertise to help problematic families. Moreover, school personnel do not have (and I see no reason why they should have) the expertise to deal with family problems.

To the extent that what is perceived as problematic in school is not, or cannot be, solved in its context (for practical, ideological, or political reasons), defining problems as individual and familial may be seen as a defensive strategy. The expert discourse *does* affect individuals and families, and if it does not help to solve problems, in turn, it certainly creates new problems. For one thing, the expert discourse can be an instrument of oppression whenever the means to solve problems satisfactorily are not available.

REDISCOVERING THE PROBLEM

Being a foreigner, one who speaks with an accent and addresses people oddly in normal situations (though White, but not self-identified with White Americans), taught me how difficult it is to live as a cultural outsider. It was not just that I did not know people and had no friends, but that all my cultural capital (education, skills, and values) was initially worth nothing. Because of my accent, peculiar manners, and speech style, I lacked face value, and was often an object of suspicion, or bluntly expected to be ignorant and inferior.

It did not take me long to learn, through afflictions and humiliations, that many Americans, even second-generation immigrants, expect Third World foreigners to defer to them. The logic (and the prevailing stereotype) seems to be that of the immigrant who left a bad situation and marvels at the goods of America. It follows that any critical attitude draws prompt antipathy, and also (as I know from experience) "a little lesson" (being scolded or advised to discard one's manners and cherished values) or punishment (being ignored or excluded). Or, perhaps, it is part of a competitive culture that one has to constantly prove oneself, as if those in power positions normally set up others within an initial frame of negative expectations. I figured I needed to work much harder than others in order to *convert* my cultural background into some sort of prevailing, conventional, local capital.

Within this context, I thought about cultural differences and conflicts, and some of their implications, particularly the price that is charged of a foreigner, or any cultural outsider, in order to participate in normal social interaction. This is especially difficult for adults who have already formed a clear adult identity. On the other hand, my children might have suffered doubly: as foreigners in their own right, and as dependent on, and thus affected by, a foreign parent mediating their interactions with others. The fact that they avoided speaking Portuguese in public and criticized my accent was not random. Interestingly, speaking a foreign language was not a sign of positive distinction or valued as cultural capital.

Parental Involvement in U.S. Schools

My encounters with the practices and discourses on home–school relations in the U.S. were influenced by my cultural background and situation as a foreign-, female-, and single-parent: the amount of homework and particular instances of *interactive homework*, the discourse on the family educational role, the typical family–school communication patterns and opportunities for parental involvement in the school, and the institution of parent education.

I understand that homework is accepted in Brazil on the grounds of a short school day, or insufficient school time that needs to be complemented at home.

Coming to the U.S., I thought my kids would attend marvelous, rich, effective, whole-day, public schools and, consequently, would never have homework. Therefore, I was quite surprised when they consistently brought schoolwork home. I was appalled when I *had* to do my part in a fifth-grade *interactive homework* assignment and *confirm* (by filling up a parent questionnaire) that I had enjoyed it! I was particularly astonished at the amount of homework during the first middle school *transition* year, and I was perplexed when my signature on a high school history homework was worth 5 extra credit points.

As a parent, I felt constrained to do *my part* in my children's homework and *enjoy* it. This was defined as my obligation by the school, and I had no choice if I did not want my kids to be low achievers, because homework substantially counted toward grades. One teacher advised parents in a school meeting not to trust children doing homework in their rooms (because they might stay quiet for hours watching TV or listening to music with headphones), and "to make sure they do it right there at the kitchen table while you fix dinner."

The show of personal satisfaction and efficiency that principals and teachers put up for parents in the open houses reminded me of private schools in Brazil. The professional aura marked those short school–family contacts, insofar as communication was usually initiated and directed by the school personnel. The purpose of those meetings was explicitly stated as to inform the parents about the goals of each course, and about their role in helping their student understand and reach them. Within such a frame, teachers' discourse toward parents invariably sounded artificial, and few teachers struck me as candid and authentic persons.

What also puzzled and annoyed me was the telephone service to inform parents that their student missed a class or a school day. My reaction was, "Of course, I know he missed school, for he stayed home—why are you informing me of something I already know and should know better than you?" I was unaware of my obligation to promptly notify the attendance office of my kid's absence, and it seemed absurd to me that the school would employ someone to do the dull job of calling parents. It took me some time to learn that this home–school communication policy revolves around responsibility for truancy and is intended to protect the school.

My first experience volunteering for a school trip to the zoo with the eighth graders was also my last of its kind. I was the only mother not to get a small group of students to chaperone and instead was put together with the seemingly most prestigious (and clearly the wealthiest) mother in the group of volunteers. Being the only foreigner, I presume I was judged incompetent to accompany a group of teenagers that included my own son.

Finally, the institution of parent education also impressed me. The very term *parenting*, and the scientific, expert definitions of *good parenting skills* taught in the workshops regularly offered by the school district suggested to me that public policy, in this country, has blatantly penetrated into the private, familial, and personal realms of life via education. Being a parent has become or is meant to become a very formal, uniform and regulated activity.

The Price of School Success

As Schutz (1964) argued, people in between two cultures are in a unique position to be analytical and critical. In the special situation of a foreign parent, I could understand the meaning of *symbolic* (or invisible) *violence*—that *innocent* exercise of power in the context of differentiated knowledge and culture in everyday social interactions. I felt imposed upon and invaded by the homework dictates; I also felt excluded and often patronized (based on stereotyped cultural assumptions) in my interactions with school personnel. It was not just that I could not pay the price to get in (learn how to socialize) and have my children get in (help them steadily with homework): I did not want to!

This is cultural resistance: I disliked being treated like an immigrant and the message it carried of having to submit to everything new and change my personality completely. However, cultural resistance should not be seen as a negative reaction that has to be simply overcome if one wants to adapt and succeed. Cultural conservatism does not mean mere stubbornness, in this case, but rather personal integrity and survival as well. It has its price too: Trying to succeed without having to adapt unilaterally and conform to the system requires of the individual, who is in the lesser power position, a great deal of (mostly unsuccessful) struggle and negotiation.

Now, putting my foreign perspective aside, there is something to be said about the meaning of homework as an invasion of family life, and as an imposition on the parent. Every time I had to participate in interactive homework or sign a homework slip, I felt like writing the teacher: "Please, don't send *me* homework!" As an adult, I do not want to submit to the teacher authority, not even for the benefit of my children, granting that the teacher knows better what is of benefit to them, and how best I should employ my time at home. To be sure, I do not want my relationship with my children to be constantly, on an everyday basis, mediated by a school topic. I do not want to talk school at home unless necessary, and I do not want to be the kind of parent who is always playing the teacher.

Moreover, I remember that when I was a student myself, I had to go through all those school subjects and tasks. So, I do not want to go through it all over again in order to *help* my children with homework, now that I am free to read and learn what I like—especially now that I know that most of the school curriculum, apart from the basics, is useless beyond granting a vague familiarity, perhaps instilling a certain scientific mentality, and allowing for college choices, in the best hypothesis. Therefore, I conceive my role as a parent (in relation to the school) as one of just encouraging (and sometimes, unfortunately, pressuring) my children to experience it all (bearing its occasional difficulty and unpleasantness), a role certainly to be shared with the teacher, whom I hope has a real passion for physics, literature, or whatever subject she or he teaches. As for the job of teaching (the school curriculum), I want to leave it entirely to the teacher, who should be well prepared and have good working conditions in order to perform well.

And, finally, there is something to be seriously pondered over the price of school success, as to whether it should amount to eliminating cultural diversity by precluding the home curriculum (the activities and conversations that make up family life and interactions) whatever it may be, and to saddling parents with the obligation to teach the school curriculum at home, when they are not prepared nor paid to do so. There is also much to be pondered about the meaning and place of *deregulated* leisure and pleasure, at least in family and private life.

Families, Cultural Diversity, and the Meaning of School

Far from home, and aging, I was flooded by memories of my childhood experiences.

I was sent to kindergarten when I was 4 years old, something unusual having a stay-home mother, and went through elementary grades in an extremely strict and repressive Catholic school. There I learned how to read and write, and had a terrorizing religious education. As I recall my home and community education, however, I can see how many alternative and diverse experiences it offered as compared to school.

I had a four-generation maternal extended family. Every Sunday evening we gathered at my grandmother's house, always full of relatives and guests, adults and children, plus dogs, cats, and a yard full of ducks and chicken. We also visited regularly my widowed great-grandmother, who lived in a townhouse with other aged relatives. In those visits, besides playing outside, children sat in the living room and listened to adults' conversations, and drank adult beverages: at my grandmother's, coffee, and at my great-grandmother's, a variety of homemade fruit liqueurs.

Our household had maids from the countryside, with whom we children had a very close, affectionate relationship. We joined many of their activities. From them we learned to plant corn, beans, collards, tomatoes, sweet potatoes, and peanuts; to make fires; to roast cashews; and to recognize snakes. In the beginning of the rainy season, at dusk, we children collected fat flying ants (*tanajuras*) on the unpaved streets that the maids would stir-fry and eat. The nutritious value of *tanajuras* was never a topic in the school curriculum. When I was 10, and dying of curiosity, one of them told me how babies were born in the most simple, straightforward way, an information denied by my mother and by the school.

I heard many stories as a child, before TV invaded homes. My grandmother told stories of animals, featuring conflicts of power, and the astuteness and tricks of the weaker, and stories of *cangaceiros*—the old bands of rural bandits in northeastern Brazil. My mother loved to tell the stories of her maternal grandfather, the character she most admired and who inspired her to study law, and of the people in his household and the sugarcane mills where she spent her vacations. My aunt Mira was a fine storyteller, who could entertain me for hours depicting life and people in the boarding school of German nuns where she had spent her school years. And the maids told tales about fantastic creatures from the woods, protectors of the forest and its animals.

Every Sunday morning my father would take us children to the movies and to the club, so that my mother could have some time alone. Back home, we would sit around the lunch table for hours, and have Greek theater for dessert, my mother's passion for a while, when she took some courses to fill her boring time as a housewife. Both my parents did amateur theater during my childhood years, and so I was frequently taken to the theater, and later to all the classic music concerts and art movies in town.

My family had a lot to offer in terms of both cultural and social capital (and of contradictions!) but they did not have a close relationship with my schools. For one thing, my mother invested her family social capital when she forced the nuns to take me—the daughter of an atheist (my father) and of a couple not married in the Roman Catholic Church—as their student. My father, who had an individual history of upward social mobility, was more likely to help with school subjects (especially math and science) at home. He had been a brilliant student and had high academic expectations for his children. However, my parents neither frequented the religious and the public schools that I attended (in the first case, because they were not part of the community, and, in the second case, because this was not a part of the school or family cultures), nor got involved with curricular issues or homework contents.

For me, school was a world apart, clearly limited and colorless, but strong in its demands. It became broader when I moved to a big secondary public school where there was much more freedom, and a variety of boys and girls to whom to relate. I often hung around with my classmates after school, walked downtown or went to the movies, and visited their families out of my neighborhood and immediate social group. This was the most interesting part of going to school!

Thus, I was educated in and through many worlds, among which school comprised an important, central, but definitely limited part. School and its work were my chief obligation, weekdays' schedules were organized around school time, but school would also function as a bridge to other activities and people, clearly disconnected from the school curriculum.

If I imagine my life as a child limited to school, and my experiences reduced to its curriculum, I can only see my life as impoverished. Moreover, I find no evidence that schools have become better, more interesting, and spiritually richer places for the education of children today, as compared to my days.

SUMMING UP

My own experience says that family–school relations and educational contexts involve an array of complex issues—social values, institutional purposes, conceptions of public and private, kinds of knowledge, forms of learning, personal meanings, views on the role of parents and teachers—and a variety of practices, all of which, moreover, bear change and diversity. Even though educational issues and practices appear tangled, it is important to keep clear that families and schools are distinct institutions, situated in different spaces and times of everyday life, comprising particular (physical and social) arrangements, responding to different social and individual needs, and carrying exclusive functions. Although children move and develop principally within and between the contexts of the two (as other forms of community have become rare), families' functions are much more complex, and families are responsible for more than school is in terms of life experiences and education in the broad sense.

Nevertheless, within present social arrangements, the most viable mediation between children and private life, as one realm, and social knowledge and the public world, as another, still is the public school, represented by the teacher, the class group, and the curriculum and mass organized activities. From this perspective, any family environment is limited, and parents are ill-equipped to exert this mediation role effectively, as they (a) mostly do not have that as their main task; (b) are disconnected from the academic world; (c) are not specialists in cognitive development, or academic subjects; (d) and have diverse kinds of public participation, and their own demanding occupations. Moreover, parents are unprepared to *help* teach the school curriculum the more specialized school content is, and the more remote it is from practical social pursuits. Attempts to connect school knowledge and everyday life are doomed to be limited, for school knowledge encompasses abstract, nontrivial, and initially noncommon knowledge.

Because school is a specialized institution of formal education, and because schooling is a big public enterprise, I see the separation of family and school, within present conditions, as (more than a functional choice) a requirement for individual freedom and cultural pluralism, and as an approach to equity. Assuring that education (as a function of the state), compulsory schooling (as preparatory for public life), and school culture (as common and necessary knowledge) remain separate from private life means allowing space for other forms of education, responsive to various human needs, to flourish apart from school. And, given that schools are also testing–credentialing institutions, limiting educational assessment to what is publicly designated as school knowledge and offered explicitly by the school might avoid the appraisal and discrimination of other cultures, making academic culture more manageable by those who are not initially socialized into it.

Along this line, one of the issues that have most impressed me in U.S. education is the extension of schooling in time, along the day and the life span, and its penetration into family life. The extraordinary development of the educational system and the race for school credentials as a means for social mobility constitute a unique U.S. phenomena, bearing upon the role of education both in Protestant ideology and in a land of immigrants, as stressed by Arendt (1961). And, indeed, it is possible to see a movement of family reform via school reform, within the formalization and normalization of parental involvement in schooling, insofar as school culture permeates everyday family practices, homogenizing the basic make up of social life.

There is concern with this policy movement toward articulating a single agenda for schools and families, in that it basically narrows the scope of conceivable educational goals and practices, while loosing sight of the specificity of public education (which cannot be conceived except in dialectical opposition to private experiences). In my view, what school and family share is a *division* of educational work and responsibility for children, the specific educational role of school being to provide for a common culture (beyond cultural diversity), a special kind of learning (systematic, skilled, refined), and knowledge (intellectual, significant, and useful for all social groups), through its specialized professionals, and unique collective environment. Obviously there are many areas of human development and many cultural contents that are not, and cannot possibly be, attended to by schools. Schools are limited. They cannot represent all the diversity of human experience. Of course, the challenge for the public school is to overcome social discrimination and exclusion based on cultural diversity. However, the present call for diversity is doubtful, as the problem of cultural pluralism cannot be solved within schools. How is cultural diversity going to be conciliated with necessarily restrictive definitions of school knowledge, and especially with valuation of knowledge and evaluation of learning?

So, I take the opposite direction of current educational policy addressing families, by assuming the perspective of the family expressed by this question: How are families going to recreate their immediate, everyday conditions of life, freely, if they are to be converted into partners of schools, guided by expert definitions, and occupied with academic goals? If schools and families represent distinct interests in terms of individual and social development, if their normal interaction comprises potential conflict as posed by Waller (1965), and if the attempt to define a common (inter-institutional) educational agenda is likely to trigger a struggle, I would bet that institutional separation is more viable than mutual involvement. The seeming intrusion of schooling into the family at this point in the history of U.S. education suggests not only that there is actual struggle over social values and definitions of academic knowledge—a struggle for cultural hegemony within the school—but also that the school detains the dominant position within that struggle in detriment of the family.

Therefore, ideally, educators and policymakers must consider family perspectives and face the issues of social purposes, knowledge, and the public character of schooling, so that schools can better account for the task of educating all children, and families can be set free to educate their children in their own ways.

3

Education and Social Reproduction: The Quest for Equity Within Family–School Relations

In this chapter, I consider possible equity implications of educational policy prescribing a family–school partnership in terms of parental involvement in schooling and parental implementation of academic activities in the home. I frame this issue according to the current rationale that parental involvement is a resource for improving individual student success, counteracting minority group failure (therefore minimizing inequity), raising educational standards and general outcomes, insuring individual and national economic competitiveness and, moreover, building family and community relations.

If the promises of education and schooling for human and social development held true, we should expect more individual achievement, enhancement and equalization of school outcomes, and increased social equality over time. Under this assumption, parental commitment to students' educational success would be natural and all parents would be positively involved with schooling. However, demographic evidence shows that school success does not happen for all and, furthermore, that successful schooling does not automatically create more social equality. In this context, parental apathy has been pointed at as an educational problem—as an actual justification of school failure—by teachers and policymakers, whereas the belief in the power of education and the function of schooling remains unexamined. Some parents' apparent neglect has appeared as a problem in comparison with a particular image of positive parental involvement—one associated with school success. In this perspective, the issue seems at once simple and intriguing: Why wouldn't all parents want the best (defined as educational and socioeconomic success) for their own children? If it is all (apparently) a matter of individual (parental) effort and commitment, how can teachers, policymakers, and researchers get parents more involved?

Even more complicated is the issue of the social purposes and outcomes of education. In 1848, Horace Mann (1957) wrote: "Education, then, beyond all other devices of human origin, is the great equalizer of the conditions of men—the balance-wheel of the social machinery" (p. 87). This is one vision of the social role of education. Another understanding is that the educational system serves to reproduce social inequalities rather than eliminating them (Bourdieu & Passeron, 1977). There are two visible actors in this drama: schools (teachers and the educational structures within which they operate) and the families (parents) of the children who attend schools. Each plays a specific role in shaping the learning outcomes, the acquisition of credentials, and the social outcomes of education, in the context of their interactions and of the larger dynamics of economic, political, social, and cultural life.

But what are the particular educational roles of school and family? According to Mann's ideal, the school, as the principal agency of education, should promote social equality despite prior individual and family differences, in which case the role of school is preponderant. As stated in the second view, the power of school has been exerted not to minimize inequality but to perpetuate it, meaning that the school operates based on family and class differences. In contrast, educational policy is now calling for the specific contribution of the family in enhancing and equalizing school outcomes, in which case the role of the family is recognized as decisive. Nevertheless, as long as either schools or families appear as more or less accountable for school success and social equality, the specific role of educational policy in shaping and regulating their interaction (and the ensuing educational and social outcomes) remains off the fray. Educational policy, as a function of the state within social organization, must therefore be assessed precisely in its power to frame the roles and interactions of school and family.

Although we have come to think of education and educational policy as restricted to school (and do not consider the private policies or politics of families), public policy touches the private and, as in the case in point, precisely articulates the roles of families and schools in social reproduction. Social reproduction is used here in the generic sense, as practices of social continuance, involving physical/material and cultural/symbolic relations, and both creation and preservation. In *Reproduction in Education, Society and Culture*, Bourdieu and Passeron (1977) defined *education* as "the process through which a cultural arbitrary is historically reproduced . . . the equivalent, in the cultural order, of the transmission of genetic capital, in the biological order" (p. 32). Although there is a common reaction against this concept as one that does not allow for human agency, I understand that social reproduction happens necessarily through human agency, that is, through productive actors (although some might be alienated from decision making, participation, or enjoyment of certain outcomes), pursuing specific goals and carrying specific practices of conservation and transformation, including individuals and institutions. Thus, educational policy deals, either implicitly or explicitly, with aims, meanings, conditions, and practices of families and schools as social institutions in defining the politics of knowledge and the social role of education.

Educational policy can be understood in numerous ways: (a) as state interventions amid social demands; (b) as generative rules and resources within social systems (Giddens, 1979); (c) as discourses–practices (Cherryholmes, 1988) within institutions or as authoritative frameworks (goals, conditions, and means) for collective action; (d) and, last, but not least, as the concrete choices of policymakers, researchers, teachers, parents, and students, whose complex combination draws courses of action that are never the automatic realization of the official agenda. If policy represents political choices, it is obviously the result of politics, both formal and informal. The term *politics* has a negative connotation in common discourse, but it can be simply defined as the practice or strategy of obtaining power or control. This definition agrees with the concept of policy: "a judgement, derived from some system of values and some assessment of situational factors, operating as a general plan for guiding decisions regarding the means of attaining desired objectives" (Good, 1973). Politics comprises two aspects: policy (calls and directives for implementation, as registered in official documents) and politics (formal and informal practices that follow or oppose, resist or recreate those directives). Therefore, educational policy can be better understood as policy–politics, for policy is more than goals and means, or frameworks and resources, insofar as it includes practices and outcomes, collective courses of action and their broad effects. Along this line, although it usually is not formulated by teachers, parents or students, formal policy is implemented or rejected, reproduced or resisted by them, and therefore its conceptualization must include practice and all of its actors, who may always, in some degree, recreate it differently than the original intentions of those who conceived it.

Policy–politics is in fact the main force within the quest for educational equity and social equality. It is necessary to stress that policies only exist as politics—as actions in pursuit of particular interests—and that agents, such as teachers, parents and students, practice politics and exercise power in intricate, asymmetric, and contradictory ways.

This stated, a few points are in order. Although both schools and families are subordinated to the state (or to the interest of a generic community in front of particular communities), they do not have equal power in the larger political context, or within the particular context of their interactions. On the one hand, the authority of an official agency (the school as a branch of the state) supersedes the prerogatives of isolated families and individuals. Thus, insofar as the school represents the state interest, it is necessarily in a position of power over families and students in enforcing policies and practices. On the other hand, the counter assertion of a two-way school–family interaction does not necessarily deny the differentials of power between family and school as social institutions, and between particular families and schools according to the class and cultural conditions of their individual members (parents and teachers)—or, as Bourdieu (1986) would say, according to the relative value of the forms of capital (economic, social, and cultural) possessed and invested by them. In other words, although it is true that family pressures have continually shaped school policy and practice, concrete specification (in time and space) is required as to which families have exerted power over schools and succeeded in shaping their educational service. Concrete specification is needed in order to prevent undue generalizations, as it is obvious that the power of families to influence school depends on both macro- and micro-sociopolitical variables, among which are included, in particular, parental educational levels and socioeconomic resources, and teachers' political and pedagogical commitments. Indeed, the power of education or school credentials has not had the same practical value for all families, therefore motivating uneven family investments in schooling.

Considering the complexities aforementioned—particularly the ostensible, monolithic, and all-pervasive political character of schools as contrasted with the diversity and dispersal of families, and the policy challenge of how best to link the educational efforts of families and schools towards the egalitarian ideal—my aim is to analyze the assumptions and implications of the current family–school partnership and parental involvement model, within a project of improvement of school outcomes. My concern is both the viability and justice of its promise. Therefore, I pursue two interrelated questions that affect the overall quality of education: How does this kind of educational policy affect different families? Is it likely to create more educational equity or inequity?

Following, I offer a reflection on some common ideas and situations, grounded in historical and sociological perspectives, and a critique of a particular policy trend—the current call for parental involvement—that frames family–school relations in problematic ways. Initially, I delineate conceptions and meanings of education, family, schooling, and family–school relations, pointing out the construction of schooling (particularly in the United States) within ideological perspectives of class, namely, social mobility and social equality. Next, I consider the specific power of schools and their limits in promoting social equality, featuring Bourdieu and Passeron's (1977) theoretical explanation of the crucial role of the educational system in the reproduction of social inequality by building on families' diverse class cultures. Finally, I discuss implications of the current educational policy framework for family–school relations, particularly for those families that do not fit its parenting model of advancing family responsibility for schooling.

I understand that current theoretical and policy formulations carry a typical middle-class bias in terms of the ideology of education for upward social mobility and consequent family adhesion to the school pedagogical project. These formulations tend to automatically benefit those families who are already cognizant of academic culture and *naturally* perform the role expected by school, while creating automatic disadvantage for families unfamiliar with school culture and unfit (by their very life conditions) to meet its expectations. Moreover, in regulating family–school relations—specifically, by defining the home as a learning setting for the school curriculum and imposing on the parents a certain educative (parenting) model—educational policy is in fact extending political regulation onto the diffuse realm of the family and private life, particularly affecting working-class and lower-class families. If this movement is to promote uniformity in family cultural and educational practices and facilitate instruction by enhancing the prior conditions of school achievement, it seems like a rather odd egalitarian strategy in aiming to correct family and social (external) differences, as well as a rather doubtful attempt to re-educate certain families, leaving the school's internal mechanisms of discrimination untouched.

Therefore, I suggest that a policy promoting parental involvement will tend to both exaggerate educational inequalities and to foster greater political subordination of family to school, penetrating and annihilating whatever diversity is left in family cultural and educational practices. It will certainly create more burdens for family life, as well as additional complications for teachers and instructional processes, pushing new demands in planning and evaluation of the articulation of home and school learning. In defining what most students and families lack or need to do in order to succeed in present school and society, and pressing families to change in order to fit the school agenda instead of trying to compensate for family educational shortcomings (defined precisely in terms of school requisites), schools (teachers, policymakers, and educational researchers) will miss the opportunity to redefine the specific educative function of schooling and broaden the meanings of education by drawing on the richness of families' diverse educational contributions.

FAMILY, SCHOOL, AND THE DEMOCRATIC IDEAL

We need to think of education, its forms and possibilities, and the educative roles of families and parents, schools and teachers, as well as other agents, within their historical and social contexts, in order to understand specific origins, evolution, and variation of practices, and the production (including change and endurance) of meanings relative to changing social needs of diverse groups. Although I do not intend to account for all of these, the picture I sketch here suggests historical, class, material, and cultural variations in modes of education, family organization, and interaction between families and schools in social reproduction. Along my elaboration I stress a few key ideas: (a) meanings of education, family, and schooling are unsettled and problematic, and related to evolving social and material arrangements; (b) within social reproduction, education and family intersect and evolve in articulation, but engender their own dynamics; (c) forms of families and education vary across time and social class; (d) families have lost their once central position in the production and reproduction of life conditions and have become subordinated, in various degrees, to institutions of work and school; (e) schooling is a function of the state, which represents the interests of the powerful social groups; (f) education today has been restricted to schooling and to its exchange value (Labaree, 1997); (g) conceptions of education and schooling are defined and carried by professionals (such as researchers, psychologists, policymakers, and teachers) entrusted with specific power over lay people (such as parents); and (h) schools were constructed within social production and reproduction as providers of a service most (working) families cannot afford but need.

Conceptual and Historical Overview

Education, as a social institution, plays a main part in cultural and social production and reproduction by creating individuals who can function autonomously according to internalized social norms and values, and adapt to specific scenarios and transformations. As intentional socialization linking generations and individuals, education consists of two dimensions: a social dimension concerned with imparting to the new generations a certain cultural heritage through the work of various institutions, and an individual dimension involving the formation of dispositions and views, and the acquisition of knowledges, abilities, and values. The individual dimension is secondary to the social dimension within the framework of objective interests and power relations, be it in the microcosmos of the family or elsewhere in the context of larger institutions or the institutional network.

Modes of education and social reproduction are historically and culturally variable and arbitrary. They represent *cultural choices*, which cannot be explained in terms of natural or rational determination, but else are grounded in and the expression of material and power relations (Bourdieu & Passeron, 1977). Both the ways of imparting and the contents of the dispositions and knowledges, which are socially valued and come to constitute the process of education (the curriculum), have varied in time and space in terms of organization and practices (where, how, for how long), contents (which knowledges become habits, skills, school subjects), agencies and agents involved (who is responsible for organization and deliverance), and target subjects (according to categories like age, gender, class, and race). We can think of education, for instance, as formal and informal; an organized social effort and individual experience; a plan implemented by an educator and conscientization via diffuse socialization and participation; the process of teaching and the experiences represented by a learner; knowledge and learning; work and leisure; performance and feeling; and as self-education and collective construction. As a multifaceted process of human learning and development taking place within social practices, across various social spaces and during all the course of individual life, education must initially be distinguished from schooling—its current predominant mode. And although there are knowledges and educational practices of different statuses, education also must be recognized as the learning that occurs through random experience and general participation in social practices. The very fact that education came to be synonymous with schooling is in itself an interesting historical and sociological phenomenon.

Historically, to educate, in the general sense of rearing or bringing up children (Williams, 1983), has not been the exclusive or main attribute either of biological parents, families, or schools. Caring for the young, imparting the culture of the social group (instructing them in modes of knowledge, production, relation, and participation), and preparing them for adult roles (war, citizenship, community, family, and work) have constituted the educative tasks of various individuals, groups, and institutions (mothers, fathers, elders, teachers, extended families, clans, neighborhood, churches, and schools) through a variety of arrangements. In primitive societies, the education of children was a community task, totally informal and merged into practical life, as it is still the case in rural areas of the Third World or in poor urban areas everywhere. In European pre-modern times, children were normally brought up by other adults rather then their biological parents. Formal education, a sign of class and cultural distinction, was a consequence of being born to the apex of the social scale. Michel de Montaigne, the French philosopher, born in 1533 in France, to a family of landlords, was first cared for by a foster family before being *ready* for formal education, which initially constituted exclusive home-tutors, and then later, from ages 6 to 13 (when he concluded his schooling), at the best college in France. This is how he expressed his feelings regarding education:

> If I had any sons I would readily wish them a fate like mine: God gave me a good father. . . . From the cradle he sent me to be suckled in some poor village of his, keeping me there until I was weaned—longer in fact, training me for the lowliest of lives among the people: Freedom consists, for a large part, in having a good-humoured belly.

> Never assume responsibility for such up-bringing yourself and even less allow your wives to do so: let boys be fashioned by fortune to the natural laws of the common people; let them become accustomed to frugal and severely simple fare, so that they have to clamber down from austerity rather than scrambling up to it. My father's humour had yet another goal: to bring me closer to the common-folk and to the sort of men who need our help. . . . And the reason why he gave me godparents at baptism drawn from people of the most abject poverty was to bind and join me to them. His plan has not turned out too badly. (Montaigne, 1993, pp. 405–406)

To a certain extent, social reproduction and education are rooted in the family because sexual and physical reproduction (the daily care of the body) are located in the home and constitute their initial conditions. According to Sanders (1995), "*education* is first used in English in the early seventeenth century to refer to rearing children by paying attention to their physical needs—in the earliest years of the child's life this meant attention to nursing" (p. 190). That is why education was originally a gendered word and work:

> *Educatio prolis* is a term that in Latin grammar calls for a female subject. It designates the feeding and nurturing in which mothers engage, be they bitch, sow, or woman. Among humans only women educate. And they educate only infants, which etymologically means those who are yet without speech. . . . Men . . . engage in *docentia* (teaching) and *instructio* (instruction). The first men who attributed to themselves educational functions were early bishops who led their flocks to the *alma ubera* (milk-brimming breasts) of Mother Church from which they were never to be weaned. This is why they, like their secular successors, call the faithful *alumni*—which means sucklings or suckers and nothing else. (Illich, cited in Sanders, 1995, pp. 187–188)

The distinction between education on the one hand, and teaching and instruction on the other, is pertinent in that it brings up a distinction between an original realm of spontaneous physical and affective relations as a context of child growth, and another realm of intentional relations providing specific training to function and do things in certain ways. While the first is a realm of silent nurturing, the second is a realm of explicit (verbal and written) control, which indeed expresses a very masculinized view of education. And although in traditional societies the first realm used to be inclusive, the second realm came to be increasingly predominant in contemporary society, with the scientificization and regulation of all aspects of everyday life.

The reorganization of education and family in modern times, in the Western world, occurred within a context of profound economic, political, social, and cultural transformation. In general lines, modernity was characterized by the advent and development of capitalist industry, democratic organization, class-based social structure, urbanization, secularization, scientific rationalization, the social and human sciences, and national school systems. Furthermore, social and cultural changes entailed the separation of public (work and politics) and private (domestic) spheres of life, the transformation of the family, which lost its productive function and became the locus of private life, and "a tendency to the fragmentation of experience, a commodification and rationalization of all aspects of life, and a speeding up of the pace of daily life" (Abercrombie, Hill, & Turner, 1994, p. 270).

Under capitalism, education and family evolved through differentiation and specialization: "Whereas the family once had reproductive, economic and educational functions, in modern societies specialized institutions of work and education have developed outside the family" (Abercrombie et al., 1994, p. 118). In contrast with its earlier sense of nursing, by the mid-17th century, "in the heart of the scientific revolution, the word [education] had expanded to include habits, manners, and intellectual concerns" (Sanders, 1995, p. 190), indicating the advent of schooling.

The remarkable historical transformation of the family, as a social institution and locus of the first education, can be traced through the evolution of the word, offered by Williams (1983). Family originally meant (from the late 14th to mid-17th centuries) *household*: "a group of servants or a group of blood-relations and servants living together in one house." In aristocratic use, it also meant a *house*: "a particular lineage or kin-group, ordinarily by descent from a common ancestor," a sense "extended to indicate a people or a group of peoples" (p. 131). Between the mid-17th and late 18th centuries, "these varying senses of lineage, household, large kin-group and small kin-group" intersected (p. 133). Since then, family became known as "a small group confined to immediate blood relations" (p. 132). In the 20th century, the distinction between nuclear family and extended family perfectly expressed the split between the household sense and the kin-group sense:

> The specialization of family to the small kin-group in a single house can be related to rise of what is now called the **bourgeois family**. But this, with its senses of household and property, relates more properly, at least until C19

[the 19th century], to the older sense. From eC19 [early 19th century] . . . we find this definition: '*the group which consists of a Father, Mother and Children is called a Family*' [italics added]; yet the fact that the conscious definition is necessary is in itself significant. Several lC17 [late 17th] and C18 [18th century] uses of family in a small kin-group sense often refer specifically to *children* [italics added] . . . where the sense of household, however, may still be present. (Williams, 1983, pp. 132–133)

The meanings of family expressed interesting class connotations. While the bourgeois family was "the isolated family as a working economic unit" (Williams, 1983, p. 133), there also appeared

> . . . a distinction between a man's *work* and his **family**: he works to support a family; the family is supported by his work. It is more probable, in fact, that the small kin-group definition, supported by the development of smaller separate houses and therefore households, relates to the new working class and lower-middle class who were defined by wage-labour: not **family** as a lineage or property or as including these, and not **family** as *household* in the older established sense which included servants, but the near kin-group which can define its social relationships, in any positive sense, only in this way. (Williams, 1983, p. 133)

As for the middle class, family "combined the strong sense of immediate and positive blood-group relationships and the strong implicit sense of property" (Williams, 1983, p. 133).

Education, in its various forms and contents, has also expressed class connotations. During pre-modern times, when formal education was mainly restricted to the dominant class, socialization and informal education through *familiarity*, and community work and life was broad and diffuse. Then, for the majority of individuals, education had a concrete content, and oral and practical culture was its vehicle. Within the modern secular trend toward social and functional differentiation and bureaucratization, families lost functions and came into relationships with "specialist organizations . . . through which they can be supplied with goods or services that they themselves no longer produce" (Bidwell, 1991, p. 190). The transformation of the mode of economic production precipitated drastic changes in family life and in the mode of education, bringing in the organization of the educational system, as we know it today:

> This story of differentiation begins with the movement of economic production out of the household, away from the control of kin-based groups and into markets. Then, in large part as a result of the economic disablement of the family, one functional activity after another is stripped from the household, moving from the primary control of the family to the control of formal organizations and their increasingly professionalized staffs. This process is very clear in the case of education. (Bidwell, 1991, p. 190)

In this context, the constitution of modern schooling is connected with the emergence of a middle class or, more precisely, with the constitution of the bourgeoisie which made use of education as a sign of distinction, by identification with the aristocracy and distance from the lower classes. Bidwell (1991) illustrated this point with the account by the social historian Lawrence Stone on the *educational revolution* during the 16th and 17th centuries in England:

> Middle-class families wanted their children to be educated, but they lacked the land and large inheritances that could support an enclosed, multifunctional household in which a child's education could be accomplished. Thus, the rise of the middle class created a market in which charitable schools were turned into grammar schools, beginning a sustained, market-driven process in which formal education became a normal, lengthening life-course stage for the bulk of the English male population. (Bidwell, 1991, p. 190)

In this way, education was separated from the household and "elite boarding schools, supported by endowments and by tuition fees from parents, came to be known as 'public' schools, in contrast to the other principal means of schooling, which was the private tutor" (Coleman, 1987, p. 32). This movement, started as early as the 14th century in England, originally inscribed the public school as an arrangement to provide collective (as opposed to individual, exclusive) instruction to boys from numerous families in a specific public (in the sense of common, shared) setting that still recreated the household in its unique regime of total living experience. However,

> . . . for all children other than those of the elite, schooling was even more fully lodged in the family. It was schooling via the household's productive activities and via a system in which children and youth learned trades, other than that of their household, in nearby households. (Coleman, 1987, p. 32)

Within the evolution of specialization of social reproduction, and the deepening chasm between public and private life, families and homes (those of the middle class being paradigmatic) were redefined within the confines of sexual, physical, and psychic reproduction, as the exclusive domain of affection and intimacy. Schools took charge of the reproduction of erudite (dominant) culture, sociopolitical values, and work training, assuming ideological and economic purposes. Gradually, as families became nuclear, secluded, and fathers and mothers left the home for the workplace, a movement that reduced their social and cultural reproductive functions, schooling grew as a systematic and extensive mode of education, and as the central context and dimension of individual development, assuming additional social and emotional goals. Moreover, with its increasingly distinctive and exclusive practices, through which special knowledges and skills were granted access and/or developed, the modern school came to constitute a stage of mediation between the private and the larger public worlds (Arendt, 1961).

The institution of a state-supported system of mass compulsory schooling in the late 19th century finally represented, according to a British historian, "the triumph of public over private influences as formative in social life and individual development; in particular, it tardily recognized the obsolescence of the educative family, its inadequacy in modern society in child care and training" (Musgrove, cited in Tyack, 1976, p. 363). A similar perspective was spoused in sociology by Durkheim (Bidwell, 1991) in terms of the superior fit of the role of school in socialization for modern life, as compared to the family. And, indeed, from both macro- and micro-perspectives, the advent of mass schooling represented a solution to social reproduction and individual education within the new urban–industrial order, substituting for the family and the near community. Concretely, the provision of schools responded to needs of caring, training, and liberation of children—a solution for both the leisure of the well-off and the exploitation of the many poor— as child labor was eradicated, ingress of the young in so-called productive work was increasingly delayed, and employment often took both fathers and mothers away from home.

However, mass compulsory schooling recreated the meaning of the public school in new and contradictory ways. On the one hand, the consolidation of liberal–democratic, industrial– capitalist states demanded social reforms, among which the creation of a national school system was strategic. Educational policy and bureaucracy originated as a systematic and permanent action of the state for provision, orientation, and supervision of the school system toward broad social ideals. The public school assumed political–ideological and economic functions related to corresponding goals of citizenship and labor force training, "driven variously by egalitarian and stratifying impulses" (Bidwell, 1991, p. 191). On the other hand, access to formal education as a means of upward (individual and class) social mobility was also an aspiration of many, based on concrete prior historical experience.

The belief in the power of education, specifically literacy, as a means of moral improvement and salvation also had historical bearings in Protestant Reformation. In the process of constitution of the modern republican states, the ideal of social equalization through education turned into one of the central tenets, along with universal suffrage, of contemporary democratic ideology. Conceived as a catalyst, education represented the means to liberate and develop human powers and to construct a just society by transforming natural inequalities and overcoming previous social hierarchies based on birthrights. In the new republican regimes of the Old World, and in the emergent nations of the New World, public education appeared as a way of precisely eliminating family and class privileges, and the extremely restricted access to the literate, erudite culture, associated with the previous aristocratic or colonial order. Individual freedom, rationality, ability, and merit became the new beliefs and values associated with liberal, economic, scientific, and technical progress; the self-made *man*, active and rational, became the model citizen.

The call of education for all, invited the lower classes into the democratic project. The ideological agenda of schooling pointed at granting access to a previously exclusive knowledge, and extending the traditional canons and the bourgeoisie's new culture to the masses, as the very condition for both sociopolitical participation and personal enjoyment. The ideology of education as the great social panacea, combining socioeconomic progress and individual social mobility, became the counterpart of compulsority, a bait into the school, the labor market, democratic life, corresponding to the aspirations of part of the lower (especially urban, working) classes to the *good* life. In a sense, the public (compulsory) school materialized a new social contract (an institutionalized exchange of interests), pretending to offer a neutral educational terrain for acquisition of a common, nonfamiliar, secular knowledge that would erase cultural and social distinctions linked to family and class, thus consolidating a new democratic order.

However, while the universalization of schooling meant democratization of formal knowledge or high culture, it also meant the imposition of one cultural form over others. While it meant access to a good from which the lower classes have been excluded, it also meant cultural uniformization via compulsory learning of an arbitrary knowledge. Furthermore, the organization and the functioning of the school system limited democratization to the lower level of schooling, and set off selection processes (based on gender, race, and class) toward its higher levels. Meritocracy, as the justification for selection and discrimination, and social mobility within tight limits and through specific cultural codes, recast the ideology of education as the main instrument of social equalization.

Therefore, the meanings of the public school were recreated by the interactions of its new diverse clientele and the specific kinds of home and social class they originated from, and the evolving organization of its enlarged, bureaucratized, horizontally and vertically differentiated, system. The social mobility meaning that the upward classes had assigned to schooling was generalized in the ideology of education as the great equalizer; yet, as curricular differentiation and inequality of outcomes advanced, both the social equalization and mobility ideals fell short of meaning in the concrete experience of many underprivileged groups.

Common and Compulsory Schooling in the United States

In the United States schooling also appeared as an extension of the family and took the form of communitarian schools organized through local initiative and control within small religious (Puritan) communities. The association of liberal capitalism and Protestantism in a *land of opportunity* caused rapid and intense educational progress "while the nation was largely rural and agricultural" (Guest & Tolnay, 1985, p. 201). Indeed, according to Tyack (1976), "even before the common-school crusade of the mid-nineteenth century and before any compulsory laws, Americans were probably in the vanguard in literacy and mass schooling among the peoples of the world" (p. 359).

The motivation for the common school movement was the need to centralize state authority over local schools, and "to find an effective substitute for the mechanisms of social control and socialization that had characterized the pre-urban and pre-industrial small stable community" (Church & Sedlak, 1976, p. 80) by instilling common values (respect for private property and authority, value of hard work) onto the lower orders or classes. Indeed, according to Church and Sedlak, the rhetoric of education for social progress (an efficient workforce) and democracy (an educated citizenry), and of the role of school in solving social problems was already present then. However, under the republican–protestant–capitalist ideology, the common school seemed to have served more a particular moral cause (not implying that moral values do not bear specific political interests and consequences) than a political–democratic enterprise, as "schooling should stress unity, obedience, restraint, self-sacrifice, and the careful exercise of intelligence" (Kaestle, 1983, p. 81). In fact, as Kaestle noted, "both gender and racial stereotypes contradicted the value placed on equality and perfectibility in native Protestant ideology, and both kept the schools from being truly *common*" (p. 89).

It is interesting to note that the very idea of a *common school* carried ambiguous connotations: a school destined to the "generality of mankind," but to the "commons, as contrasted with lords and nobility" (Williams, 1983, pp.70–71), as well, according to the etymology of the word *common*. "The tension of these two senses has been persistent. Common can indicate a whole group or interest or a large specific and subordinate group" (Williams, p.71). Even in the sense of generality, it carries the same tension and a derogatory meaning:

> Common can be used to affirm something shared or to describe something *ordinary* (itself ambivalent, related to *order* as series or sequence, hence *ordinary*—in the usual course of things, but also to *order* as rank, social and military, hence *ordinary*—of an undistinguished kind); or again, in one kind of use, to describe something *low* or *vulgar* (which has specialized in this sense from a comparable origin, *vulgus*, Latin—the common people). (Williams, 1983, p. 71)

Therefore, the common (in the sense of ordinary, second order) local schoolhouses contrasted, from the beginning, with the higher quality, exclusive, elite boarding schools, that continued to serve the wealthy.

The peculiarity of the educational development in the United States was that schools were created by local, parental initiative. From 1850 to 1890, following the common school movement, schooling evolved with minimal coercion by the states, consistently with the liberal creed. Apparently, there was no need to enforce the existing compulsory attendance laws and, besides, compulsion contradicted parental rights. According to Tyack (1976), who called this first period in the history of compulsory school attendance in the United States the *symbolic stage*, there is evidence to suggest that the enactment of compulsory education laws came merely to formalize what was already an accomplished fact.

But the beliefs in the value of education also had an economic appeal. Horace Mann (1957), who had claimed that "nothing but universal education can counter-work this tendency to the domination of capital and the servility of labor"

(p. 86), also offered an economic justification for greater investment in schooling. Anticipating human capital theory, he argued that schooling contributed economic benefits both to society as a whole (through greater productivity), and to individuals (through greater earnings), and that uneducated individuals were "economic burdens to the community" (Tyack, 1976, pp. 378, 382). Moreover, he claimed that education "made workers punctual, industrious, frugal, and too rational to cause trouble for their employers" (Tyack, 1976, p. 378). Later, in the 1880s, "a committee of the United States Senate which took testimony on 'the relations between labor and capital' found that businessmen and employees across the nation tended to agree that schooling increases the productivity and predictability of workers" (Tyack, 1976, p. 379).

By the end of the 19th century, the liberal, laissez-faire capitalist venture had created new and enormous social problems, due to periodical crises in production, expansion, shifts and relocations of the wage labor force, and overpopulation in the cities. While new monopolist arrangements took shape at the economic level, a strong regulative state materialized in various extensive social reforms aimed at national consolidation via the incorporation of the new urban masses, including the new immigrants. The need to form *citizens* (in the sense of subjects of the republican state), by teaching a common language, a national history and ideology, thus breaking with the diverse loyalties to families and ethnic groups, religions and regions, and other interest groups, clearly appeared at that moment as a crucial political role of education and schooling, especially in a country where the school system had to come to grips with localism and religious conflicts, particularly among various Protestant denominations and Catholicism.

The effective institution of compulsory schooling in the United States is associated with various complex factors. On the one hand, "waves of immigration intensified the concern over the incorporation of new groups into the polity" (Tyack, 1976, p. 366). On the other hand, according to Bowles and Gintis (1976), the expansion of schooling also responded to labor–capital conflicts, as extreme exploitation of workers and concentration of wealth aroused labor militancy and claims for educational access. Said Tyack (1976):

> Advocates of compulsory schooling often argued that families—or at least some families, like those of the poor or foreign-born—were failing to carry out their traditional functions of moral and vocational training. Immigrant children in crowded cities, reformers complained, were leading disorderly lives, schooled by the street and their peers more than by Christian nurture in the home. Much of the drive for compulsory schooling reflected an animus against parents considered incompetent to train their children. Often combining fear of social unrest with humanitarian zeal, reformers used the power of the state to intervene in families and to create alternative institutions of socialization. (p. 363)

Thus, the function of *political socialization* had a clear nativist intent combined with ethnic and religious bias. Compulsory school meant to impart the *pietist* American character onto "the emigrant, the freedman, and the operative" (Tyack, 1976, p. 372).

It is also plausible that, in practice, school came to assume a function of socialization for urban life and for the new conditions of work, rather than of dissemination of *high culture*, a culture that was produced and reproduced in life conditions very different than those of the masses. Therefore, social efficiency became a basic goal expressed as social (more than intellectual) discipline: teaching the future workers the attitudes adequate to the novel mode of production that required a steady, regular, daily rhythm of work, one very different from those of the peasants or autonomous craftsmen (Bowles & Gintis, 1976). After all, the great social challenges of the time were in the economic realm, specifically in the incorporation of workers and immigrants into the new economic arrangements, preventing social dissension and turmoil.

In this context, "laws compelling school attendance were only part of an elaborate and massive transformation in the legal and social rules governing children" (Tyack, 1976, p. 363). The definition of the needs of children (typically by middle-class professionals) is closely connected to political definitions of economic and social needs, insofar as children incarnate the possibilities of social reproduction. By then, the state had clearly assumed a *parental role*, as the Supreme Court of Illinois proclaimed in 1901:

> The natural rights of a parent to the custody and control of his infant child are subordinate to the power of the State. . . . One of the most important natural duties of the parent is his obligation to educate his child, and this duty he owes not to the child only, but to the commonwealth. If he neglects to perform it, or willfully refuses to do so, he may be coerced by law to execute such civil obligation. The welfare of the child and the best interests of society require that the state shall exert its sovereign authority to secure to the child the opportunity to acquire an education. (Cited in Grubb & Lazerson, 1982, p. 25)

Then, as now, the notion of the right of every human being to education—meaning literacy and formal education—finds its antithesis in the institution of compulsory schooling in the name of constructing citizenship. To that right corresponds both the obligation of the state to guarantee equal opportunities by providing a single good quality school for all, and the obligation of the individual and the family to take such opportunities and put them to best use in order to accomplish both individual and social benefits, according to a tacit social contract. On the one hand, notions of individual advancement, social mobility, economic productivity, and social stability are implicit in the democratic ideal. On the other hand, the right of access to valued universal knowledge and techniques may eventually be the object of coercion in the name of the protection of children and in the interest of consolidation of the social order. In fact, compulsory schooling came to be required for those who did not see the value of education or who were recalcitrant.

Therefore, in the United States, the striking belief in the power of education, with all its economic and cultural connotations, and the typical (Protestant) call for effort and self-improvement, both justified and continues to justify the upward mobility of some groups (mainly White Protestant, but also Jews, and more recently Asians) in detriment of others (Black, Hispanic, and other ethnic minorities), and the imposition of specific practices of acculturation—variably called salvation, character reformation, liberation, empowerment, or else, from another perspective, colonization, domestication, oppression—over poor, disenfranchised groups. Moreover, it is clear that there are two distinct histories of education related to social class: One in which a class has created and seized the value of schooling within a particular (utilitarian) conception of education, and another in which schooling, a nonfamiliar kind of education, has been imposed upon a class as a means of salvation. The former is the history of the credentialing system while the latter is the history of socioeconomic exclusion and school failure that continues to feed on the various policies of "organized child saving" (Cravens, 1993, p. 3), currently directed to the so-called *at-risk* students.

Functional Differentiation in the Constitution of the Educational System

Tyack (1976) called the second period in the history of compulsory school attendance in the United States, starting at the turn of the 20th century, the *bureaucratic stage*. "School systems grew in size and complexity, new techniques of bureaucratic control emerged, ideological conflict over compulsion diminished, strong laws were passed, and school officials developed sophisticated techniques to bring truants into school" (p. 359). Under a "corporate model of governance" (p. 373), the movement toward centralization created city boards and state departments of education, enforcing uniform educational standards. Gradually, throughout the first half of the 20th century, mass education reached the secondary school.

Tyack (1976) also suggested that the structural differentiation of the schools developed as an intrinsic part of the machinery of compulsion:

> Schools developed not only new ways of finding children and getting them into school, but also new institutions or programs to cope with the unwilling students whom truant officers brought to their doors: parental schools, day-long truant schools, disciplinary classes, ungraded classes and a host of specialized curricular tracks. (p. 374)

The "rational expansion and functional specialization of the schools" was informed by the scientific paradigm of technical rationality, and the human sciences—psychology and the new *educational science*—played an important role in justifying the new reforms. Interestingly, "advocates of these new forms of governance argued that education should be taken out of politics and that most decisions were best made by experts" (Tyack, 1976, pp. 373–374).

A word about the larger social context is in order. According to Coontz (1992), education policy was part of a concerted—and moralist—effort in social policy aimed at "keeping families together" (p. 134), particularly those of the poor and immigrant. Thus, while "public schools extended the length of childhood in the working class" (p. 137), progressive welfare and legal reforms expanded the government "tools for monitoring, regulating, and fine-tuning their home lives" (p. 134). Contradictorily, "progressives multiplied the means available to courts and state workers for imposing middle-class norms on nonconforming families even while they instituted important humanitarian reforms and protections for women and youth" (p. 134).

At the same time, within the process of school structural differentiation and functional specialization, and probably as a result of the consolidation of the distinct process of middle-class schooling, a movement toward a *new school* took shape (attuned with a particular middle-class educational culture), reaching its apex in the second decade of the 20th century.

Liberal educators strongly publicized the need to revise traditional educational principles and practices and to create a new pedagogy destined to spiritually elevate human beings and convert school into an instrument of peace and democracy. The attack on traditional schooling focused on its nondemocratic character, teachers' verbalism, and the imposition of a static knowledge on the students. In turn, Progressive Education was based on the emergent psychological knowledge of child development, and aimed at shifting the unilateral act of teaching into active participation of the students in the process of learning. Considering students' diversity of backgrounds, conditions, inclinations, and aspirations, the new methods would focus on the act of learning, and attend simultaneously to the individual's unique conditions of development, and to differences across individuals—quite a new challenge for mass education.

What occurred, then, was a contradictory "amalgamation of democratic ideals and bureaucratic techniques" (Higham, cited in Tyack, 1976, p. 375). There was a striking historical convergence, expressed in the new curricular and pedagogical arrangements, between a conception of liberal–democratic education concerned with individual needs, and the function of differentiation school was called to perform. The outcome was the creation of a unique curricular *choice* system, based on *natural* intelligence or talent, and effort or merit. Indeed, the American solution for educational democratization is unparalleled—the system embraces all and comports everyone but grants differentiated experiences and outcomes. Gagnon (1995) called this system one of "different but equal schools," which is more encompassing than the "separate but equal" racist system, and has well survived it (p. 71).

Bowles and Gintis (1976) explained educational expansion and progressivism as an attempt to control workers by improving social conditions and inhibiting conflict, while legitimating and perpetuating the capitalist social relations of production. They argued that school performed a critical role in regulating social and economic crises, through its very expansion and differentiation, amplifying access but providing differentiated and hierarchized school curricula corresponding to the productive requirements of an increasingly segmented labor force. In this process, all are accommodated, but differential treatment based on sex and ethnicity concretely separates and alienates low class students. Ultimately, the rhetoric of equality of opportunities through education rationalizes unequal educational outcomes, further converted in unequal income and status, justifying prior social inequalities.

Thus, the horizontal and vertical expansion of the educational system provided for a continual and ever more complicated "mass triage," based on race, social class, ethnicity, language, sex, *deportment*, and intelligence (as measured by tests), all apparently originated in family conditions (Gagnon, 1995). It did away with the idea of a common education, in various aspects and degrees, with respect to access to valued knowledge. In this way, schooling became the great symbolic institutional mechanism of recomposition of social hierarchies in a rapid-pace changing society.

EDUCATION AND SOCIAL INEQUALITY

What has schooling accomplished for the entire society and for its diverse groups so far? The development of schooling in the United States is perhaps the most illustrative case of tremendous social equalization in terms of access, and extreme social differentiation, in terms of school conditions (both material and curricular) and individual and group outcomes. Indeed, as much as educational access expanded at all levels, comparative assessment of levels of attainment across sex, ethnicity, linguistic background or style, and social class has shown patterns of differentiated outcomes related to these categories. Open access has not meant equality of opportunities and conditions in the first place, insofar as horizontal differentiation of the quality of school and curricular experiences has followed, as exemplified by racial segregation, tracking, and striking contrasts between wealthy suburban schools and depleted inner-city schools (Anyon, 1981; Kozol, 1991; Oakes, 1986; Rist, 1970). But even where students presumably enjoy equal opportunities, differentiated outcomes are produced through complex and subtle processes within the school's workings, through the interaction of students' prior cultural and individual traits with those that characterize the school's knowledge/discourse and norms/practices (Cadzen, 1988; Heath, 1983; Keddie, 1971; Mehan, Hertweck, & Meihls, 1986; Michaels, 1986). Furthermore, the vertical expansion of the system has also preserved the rarity of higher education experiences and credentials for a restricted group (Labaree, 1997). Overall, increasingly higher levels of general educational attainment have not affected basic social hierarchies or made a significant difference in minimizing social inequalities.

In the 1960s, following the Civil Rights Act of 1964, an extensive survey was carried out in order to assess inequalities of educational opportunity for ethnic minority groups in the U.S. educational system. Known as the Coleman Report

(Coleman et al., 1966), its findings revealed that the achievement of the average Native American, Mexican American, Puerto Rican, and African American (in descending order) was much lower than that of the average White and Asian American in Grades 1, 3, 6, 9, and 12, as measured by standardized tests. In effect, "at the beginning of the twelfth grade, these groups were, on the average, three, four, or five grade levels behind Whites in reading comprehension, and four, five, or six grade levels behind in mathematics achievement" (Coleman, 1967, p. 21). But the survey also indicated that:

> . . . within broad geographic regions, and for each racial or ethnic group, the physical and economic resources going into a school had very little relation to the achievement coming out of it; . . . variations in teacher salaries, library facilities, laboratories, school size, guidance facilities had little relation to student achievement—when the family backgrounds of the students were roughly equated. (Coleman, 1967, p. 21)

Moreover, the "strong relation of family economic and educational background to achievement" increased over the school years: "At the end of school, the conditional probabilities of high achievement are even *more* conditional upon racial or ethnic background than they are at the beginning of school" (Coleman, 1966, p. 73).

Coleman (1966) interpreted these findings in the following terms:

> (1) these minority children have a serious educational deficiency at the start of school, which is obviously not a result of school; and (2) they have an even more serious deficiency at the end of school, which is obviously in part a result of school. (Coleman, 1966, pp. 72–73)

> Altogether, *the sources of inequality of educational opportunity appear to lie first in the home itself and the cultural influences immediately surrounding the home; then they lie in the schools' ineffectiveness to free achievement from the impact of the home, and in the schools' cultural homogeneity which perpetuates the social influences of the home and its environs.* (Coleman, 1966, pp.73–74)

The determining weight of the educational and economic resources provided by the home was also evidenced in the connection between school social environment (resulting from family background) and variation in achievement across schools, in the specific context of racial, class, and cultural homogeneity of both the student and teacher bodies of U.S. schools:

> Per pupil expenditure, books in the library, and a host of other facilities and curricular measures show virtually no relation to achievement if the *social environment* of the school—the educational backgrounds of other students and teachers—is held constant. (Coleman, 1966, p. 73)

Given this homogeneity, "the principal agents of effectiveness in the schools—teachers and other students—act to maintain or reinforce the initial differences imposed by social origins" (Coleman, 1966, p. 73). Whereas "homogeneity works to the disadvantage of those children whose family's educational resources are meagre" (Coleman, 1967, p. 22), heterogeneity aids achievement: "students do better when they are in schools where their fellow students come from backgrounds strong in educational motivation and resources. . . . This effect appears to be particularly great for students who themselves come from educationally-deprived backgrounds" (p. 21).

Therefore, the policy challenge then was to simultaneously desegregate the schools (promoting cultural heterogeneity), and to provide equal opportunity for educational performance (raising the achievement of minority groups):

> In some part, the difficulties and complexity of any solution derive from the premise that our society is committed to overcoming not merely inequalities in the distribution of educational *resources*, but inequalities in the opportunity for educational achievement. This is a task far more ambitious than has ever been attempted by any society: not just to offer, in a passive way, equal access to educational resources, but to provide an educational environment that will free a child's potentialities for learning from the inequalities imposed upon him by the accident of birth into one or another home and social environment. (Coleman, 1967, pp. 20–21)

On the one hand, Coleman (1966) recognized the need to make the educational program of the school more effective, for "the weakness of this program is apparent in its inability to overcome initial differences" (p. 74). Along this line, he stated that "equality of educational opportunity implies, not merely *equal* schools, but equally *effective schools, whose influences will overcome the differences in starting point of children from different social groups*" (p. 72, italics added), pointing at equality of outcomes. On the other hand, he was cautious to say that

> . . . the only kinds of policies that appear in any way viable are those which do not seek to improve the education of Negroes and other educationally disadvantaged at the expense of those who are educationally advantaged. This implies new kinds of educational institutions, with a vast increase in expenditures for education—not merely for the disadvantaged but for all children. (Coleman, 1966, p. 74)

Indeed, Coleman proposed a very ingenious solution—the *open school*, which I address subsequently. Yet, he did not say how it would be possible to overcome disadvantages while maintaining advantages, that is, without any specific costs for the advantaged or redefinition of the very meaning of advantage.

The Role of the Family in the Production of School Outcomes: The Cultural Deficit Model

By calling minority children's background knowledge and home experiences "a serious educational deficiency" (Coleman, 1966, p. 72), and by referring to their "educationally-deprived backgrounds" (Coleman, 1967, p. 21), Coleman clearly adopted the cultural deficit view. According to this view, the ways of life of those who do not belong to a particular (hegemonic) culture are not legitimate and, therefore, are not even recognized as a distinct culture. Likewise, it does not recognize any other form of education different from the formal learning of the subjects and sentiments, historically constructed by the dominant classes, which comprise schooling. An alternative view contemplates diverse cultures and respective modes of education within power relations, so that White schooled individuals, for instance, could be considered deficient in Ebonics, or deprived of certain knowledges foreign to their lifestyle, if the power–race equation were different. Because White schooled individuals, within prevalent social relations, have nothing to lose by not speaking Ebonics or by ignoring a variety of knowledges typical of the experiences of oppressed groups, they tend to be blind to (as they find themselves in a comfortable position to deny) the culture and the mode of education of those groups.

By stating that "the sources of inequality of educational opportunity appear to lie first in the home itself and the cultural influences immediately surrounding the home" (Coleman, 1966, pp.73–74), and curiously conceiving the home as a setting of *educational opportunity*, Coleman did not explicitly distinguish between an institution (school) expressly entrusted with the political function of providing educational opportunity and another (family) that cannot be properly defined in terms of this function. Thus, whereas sources of social inequality *lie* in the home and its environs, and inequalities (previously produced) are originally "imposed . . . by the accident of birth into one or another home and social environment" (Coleman, 1967, p. 21), sources of inequality of educational opportunity *are produced* at school (e.g., ability grouping, tracking), and *not by accident*.

In other words, original social inequality is reproduced through the production of educational opportunities of a certain kind, either through the provision of differentiated opportunities (again, tracking), or of equal opportunities for individuals who are not equally able to take advantage of them. To attribute to the family the function of providing educational opportunity (specifically an education of a certain kind), when families vary in their economic and educational conditions, means making them responsible for the fate of children across the other institutions of a very complex society; to recognize the incapacity of families (prey of social inequality) to provide equal education (the argument for compulsory schooling), means to establish their dependency upon effective schools. Hence, it is one thing to conceive of the school as the institution that mediates between original social *(family)* inequality and the construction of social equality or inequality, and another thing, quite unrealistic and unfair, to imply that the family should exert such a mediation role defeating social inequality. In fact, as Lareau (1993) demonstrated empirically, upper middle-class families are the ones that exert an active mediation role within the interaction between their children's individual traits and the school format, precisely because they are in a condition to do so.

Coleman's discourse assumed specific conceptions of school and family, and a precise type of family–school relations: "The schools were once seen as a supplement to the family in bringing a child into his place in adult society, and they still function largely as such a supplement, merely perpetuating the inequalities of birth" (Coleman, 1966, p. 75). In this way, Coleman recognized the role of schools in reproducing social inequalities by functioning as "a supplement to the family"—a setting in which a family's standing is projected, advanced, fortified, continued— "in bringing a child into his place in adult society," into a predetermined place within a static social project. Yet, according to the dominant cultural framework, insofar as he viewed the school as the legitimate extension of a particular type (but the only desirable model) of family, that is, the typical White middle-class family, he assigned families responsibility for school effectiveness or ineffectiveness.

How could schools function differently, in order to promote equality of educational opportunities and outcomes? Despite rhetorical ambiguities, in the 1960s, Coleman offered a radical policy solution, a whole systemic reform, which interestingly anticipated many of the reform attempts that followed.

In order to attend to the specific backwardness of minority achievement, and consonant with the deficit view, Coleman (1966) proposed the substitution of the home environment of the educationally deprived by larger amounts of schooling:

> For those children whose family and neighborhood are educationally disadvantaged, it is important to replace this family environment as much as possible with an educational environment—by starting school at an earlier age, and by having a school which begins very early in the day and ends very late. (p. 74)

What is basically required for special programs targeted at minorities, in order to improve the education of the disadvantaged at minimum cost for the advantaged, are funds—"the solutions might be in the form of educational parks, or in the form of private schools paid by tuition grants (with Federal regulations to insure racial heterogeneity), public (or publicly subsidized) boarding schools" (Coleman, 1966, p. 74)—whereas the whole educational mode and the meaning of advantage associated to it remain untouched.

Coleman also stressed the importance of attitudes for minorities (the feeling of control of one's own fate, the belief in effort over luck) in overcoming obstacles, revealing a choice of individual and symbolic factors (personal qualities) over social and material factors (institutional and economic constraints), as well as blindness to the stronger, original determination of the latter group of factors, within their mutual interaction, in the explanation of the construction of inequality:

> Those Negroes who gave responses indicating a sense of control of their own fate achieved higher on the tests than those whites who gave the opposite responses. This attitude was more highly related to achievement than any other factor in the student's background or school. . . . The determination to overcome relevant obstacles, and the belief that he will overcome them . . . may be the most crucial elements in achieving equality of opportunity. (Coleman, 1966, p. 75)

But the reduction of the social and racial homogeneity of the school environment was (and still is) quite a challenge. Coleman (1967) saw obstacles in institutions like the neighborhood school and tracking, and argued that "heterogeneity of race and heterogeneity of family educational background can increase the achievement of children from weak educational backgrounds with no adverse effect on children from strong educational backgrounds" (p. 22). However, and equally consonant with the dominant cultural framework, he conceived equity only within cultural homogeneity, implying that cultural heterogeneity (in the classroom) was merely a strategy to build cultural homogeneity (i.e., an opportunity for students from diverse backgrounds to acquire the right kind of education). Moreover, because educationally strong middle-class students were the prototype and the model to be followed (hence the need that they be in greater numbers in order to influence the educationally weak), he found a peculiar difficulty in desegregating schools and classrooms: "there are simply not enough middle class children to go around" (p. 22).

On the other hand, albeit vaguely, Coleman (1966) pointed to the need to make the educational program of the school more effective by reorganizing the curriculum within schools and adopting new instructional methods:

> One of the major reasons for "tracking" is the narrowness of our teaching methods—they can tolerate only a narrow range of skill in the same classroom. Methods which greatly widen the range are necessary to make possible racial and cultural integration within a school—and thus to make possible the informal learning that other students of higher educational levels can provide. (pp. 74–75)

Nevertheless, he seemed to find school reform limited in face of social inequality of students' backgrounds: "Thus, a more intense reconstruction of the child's social environment than that provided by school integration is necessary to remove the handicap of a poor family background" (Coleman, 1967, p. 23). Therefore, the solution he envisioned was a radical and inventive school choice system: *open schools* as centers of operations toward the two goals of achievement and integration.

Coleman's (1967) model conciliated state control, free initiative, social efficiency, and consumer choice. *Open schools* were "a home-base that carries out some teaching functions but which serves principally to coordinate [students'] activities and to perform guidance and testing functions" (p. 24). The teaching of each subject matter:

. . . would be opened up to entrepreneurs outside the school, under contract with the school system . . . and paid on the basis of increased performance by the [students] on standardized tests. . . . The payment-by-results would quickly eliminate the unsuccessful contractors, and the contractors would provide testing grounds for innovations that could subsequently be used by the school. (Coleman, 1967, p. 25)

While some schools would outlast the competition, others might lose most of their teaching functions: "The contract centers [would] provide the school with a source of innovation as well as a source of competition to measure its own efforts, neither of which it has had in the past" (Coleman, 1967, p. 27). Parental choice would be a key element of the model: "The school would find it necessary to compete with the system's external contractors to provide better education, and the parent could, for the first time in education, have the full privileges of consumer's choice" (p. 25), "as well as the opportunity to help establish special purpose programs" (p. 27). To overcome the problem of racial and class segregation, classes and activities would be organized on a cross-school basis, with students from different home-base schools gathering as members of the same team or club in a variety of interscholastic academic events. Community organizations would also be able to act as contractors, offering cultural enrichment and community action programs involving students from several schools and diverse class and ethnic backgrounds, according to the free choice of parent or student. Finally, state control would prevent resegregation along racial or class lines in the organization of the contracted-classes by regulating enrollment, and would maintain the common standards "always with the public school establishing the criteria for achievement, and testing the results" (p. 26).

One interesting aspect of this model was the downsizing of the educational bureaucracy, limiting it to the control of educational *outcomes*, while parental control would focus on the educational *process* with ample choice of methods, but not of the tested contents. Coleman (1967) recognized that the public educational system is a monopoly where consumers lack free choice and, therefore, can only exercise their interest through organized power, but he seemed to suggest that a better locus of consumer organized power may be found outside the educational system. Ultimately, he diverted the focus from issues of curricular content, school knowledge, and culture.

The Role of the Educational System in the Reproduction of Social Inequality: Social Reproduction Through Cultural Reproduction

Let us review Coleman's fundamental questions: Why are schools ineffective to free achievement from the impact of the home? How can schools reduce the dependence of a child's opportunities upon his social origins?

In the 1970s, theories of social reproduction through education—presenting a macro, social-structural view—and theories of cultural production—focusing on micro, institutional processes of cultural imposition and individual and group processes of opposition and resistance (Willis, 1977)—offered challenging accounts of the *reproduction* of social inequality through and within schools.

The most encompassing and original sociological approach to the role of the educational system in the reproduction of social inequality—and, more generally, the intersection of capitalist schooling, symbolic production, and domination—has been offered by Bourdieu and Passeron (1977) in *Reproduction in Education, Society and Culture*, and further elaborated by Bourdieu (1977, 1986). In these works, they present rich possibilities to think of social practices as power-charged symbolic exchanges within the simultaneous play of class and individual, objective and subjective, systemic and personal interests, and to envision education as symbolic violence (necessarily including cultural imposition, discrimination, and exclusion), and as a main site of production of (class) cultural hegemony. Therefore, they allow us to understand that the problem of inequality of educational opportunities and outcomes is not enclosed by the actions and interactions of individuals, schools, and families, but is broadly inscribed into cultural struggles rooted in (class) economic competition.

Reading these dense theoretical pieces (based, nevertheless, on empirical sociological research) is quite an effort, due to their style, characterized by extreme conceptual rigor combining comprehension, specificity and precision of language (originally French). And writing about these theories, that is, paraphrasing them, is quite a challenge because one runs the risk of losing crucial meanings while trying to simplify them. Therefore, in order to be faithful, the use of long quotations is practically unavoidable, which I do extensively in a patchwork manner of re-construction.

Briefly, Bourdieu and Passeron (1977) explained school's ineffectiveness to free achievement from the impact of the home in terms of its effectiveness to reproduce social inequality based on family and class cultural differences. Bourdieu (1986) framed the specific role of the school in the reproduction of class hierarchies within the complex interplay of various forms of symbolic and economic capital across family, school, and market. Finally, Bourdieu and Passeron (1977) and Bourdieu (1977) indicated how cultural and class reproduction works pedagogically and how the school and the teacher keep its cycle.

The cycle of cultural and social *re-production* articulates individuals and structures within capital exchanges and conversions: Symbolic and economic forms of capital, initially available in the home environment, produce and reproduce the cultural capital (valued knowledge and skills), which is further developed in school and converted into educational credentials, which in turn are exchanged by social and economic capital (jobs and income), according to the broader rules of the market. In this cycle, the modern educational system plays a specific role in the "reproduction of the structure of power relationships and symbolic relationships between classes, by contributing to the reproduction of the structure of the distribution of cultural capital among these classes." Rather than promoting equity or social mobility, the educational system provides a *solution* "to the problem of the transmission of power and privileges . . . by contributing to the reproduction of the structure of class relations and by concealing, by an apparently neutral attitude, the fact that it fills this function" (Bourdieu, 1977, pp. 487–488).

Thus, the function of cultural reproduction proper to all educational systems is connected to their function of social reproduction: Cultural reproduction legitimates the fact of economic and class reproduction. This happens in the following way:

> . . . the different pedagogic actions . . . carried out by families from the different social classes as well as that which is practised by the school [do not] work together in a harmonious way to transmit a cultural heritage which is considered [by classical theories] as being the undivided property of the whole society. . . . In fact . . . the inheritance of cultural wealth which has been accumulated and bequeathed by previous generations only really belongs (although it is *theoretically* offered to everyone) to those endowed with the means of appropriating it for themselves. In view of the fact that the apprehension and possession of cultural goods as symbolic goods (along with the symbolic satisfactions which accompany an appropriation of this kind) are possible only for those who hold the code making it possible to decipher them or, in other words, that the appropriation of symbolic goods presupposes the possession of the instruments of appropriation, it is sufficient to give free play to the laws of cultural transmission for cultural capital to be added to cultural capital and for the structure of the distribution of cultural capital between social classes to be thereby reproduced. (Bourdieu, 1977, p. 488)

The process of education, or internalization of cultural capital, initiated in the family environment, consists of "the production of the *habitus*, that system of dispositions which acts as a mediator between structures and practice" (Bourdieu, 1977, p. 487). The school builds upon a prior particular habitus, hence legitimating a certain kind of family cultural capital. It follows that the action of the educational system is most effective the more it involves individuals who have enjoyed a prior familiarity with the symbolic wealth that constitutes *legitimate* culture in their family upbringing. In this way,

> . . . the educational system reproduces all the more perfectly the structure of the distribution of cultural capital among classes (and sections of a class) in that the culture which it transmits is closer to the dominant culture and that the mode of inculcation to which it has recourse is less removed from the mode of inculcation practised by the family. (Bourdieu, 1977, p. 493)

In effect, the school at once ensures a cultural monopoly and benefits those families that are capable of transmitting, by their own means, the instruments necessary for the reception of its message.

The problem for lower class families and their students is that, while they lack the cultural capital necessary to take advantage of educational opportunities, the school precisely fails to explicitly transmit the means of appropriation of the dominant culture, thereby creating the opportunity for their acquisition of educational credentials—and, hopefully, for the development of critical consciousness. As Bourdieu (1977) explained:

> ... the educational system never succeeds quite so completely in imposing recognition of its value and of the value of its classifications [credentials] as when its sanctions are brought to bear upon classes or sections of a class which are unable to set against it any rival principle of hierarchical ordering. (p. 504)

In this way, lower class students tend to fail in the formally neutral academic market, and the school system ends up reinforcing and consecrating initial social inequalities.

On top of that, said Bourdieu (1977), academic credentials depend on the objective sanctions of a market dominated by the symbolic products of the educational work of the families of the dominant classes, who also hold the monopoly of the most prestigious schools. In reality, academic capital (a form of cultural capital) is a weak currency that depends on the economic and social capital that can be put to its valorization. So, whereas the academic investments of the ruling classes cannot fail to be extremely profitable, the diploma is utterly indispensable for those from families less favored in economic and social capital. Therefore, the educational system enjoys little real autonomy, exerting mainly a function of legitimization by converting social hierarchies into educational hierarchies, in this way anticipating the objective sanctions of the symbolic and economic market.

The specificity of the pedagogical action of the school—the conversion of the primary *habitus* into knowledges and skills exchangeable for formal qualifications or credentials—is further explained:

> [As the mastery] ... of the available instruments of appropriation and, more specifically, of the generic and particular code of the work [of art, or any cultural object, is] the necessary condition for the deciphering of the work, ... in the specific case of works of "high" culture, mastery of the code cannot be totally acquired by means of the simple and diffuse apprenticeships provided by daily existence but presupposes an education methodically organized by an institution specially equipped for this purpose. It is to be noted, however, that the yield of pedagogic communication, entrusted, among other functions, with the responsibility of transmitting the code of works of "high" culture, along with the code according to which this transmission is carried out, is itself a function of the cultural competence that the receiver owes to his family upbringing, which is more or less close to the "high" culture transmitted by the colleges and to the linguistic and cultural models according to which this transmission is carried out. (Bourdieu, 1977, p. 493)

In summary, the possible contribution of schooling to social equalization— that is, the provision of equality of educational opportunity for social and economic advancement—is restricted initially by the very cultural–pedagogical processes, which produce unequal school outcomes, and further by the market-driven relation between educational credentials and economic and social rewards:

> The laws of the market which fixes the economic or symbolic value, i.e. the value qua cultural capital, of the cultural arbitraries produced by the different pedagogic actions and thus of the products of those pedagogic actions (educated individuals), are one of the mechanisms—more or less determinant according to the type of social formation—through which social reproduction, defined as the reproduction of the structure of the relations of force between the classes, is accomplished. (Bourdieu & Passeron, 1977, p. 11)

Ultimately, the school is nothing but a specific setting of social and symbolic exchanges and circulation of cultural capital in a society marked by differentiated distribution of material and symbolic resources.

Symbolic Capital

In "The Forms of Capital," Bourdieu (1986) proposed the expansion of the concept of capital to include various symbolic forms, also liable to "accumulation and all its effects" (p. 241). He claimed that the understanding of the logic of capital requires that two opposing views be superseded: "economism, which, on the grounds that every type of capital is reducible in the last analysis to economic capital, ignores what makes the specific efficacy of the other types of capital, and . . . semiologism (nowadays represented by structuralism, symbolic interactionism, or ethnomethodology), which reduces social exchanges to phenomena of communication and ignores the brutal fact of universal reducibility to economics" (pp. 252–253).

Thus, he developed the concepts of *cultural and social capital*, "transformed, disguised forms of economic capital" (p. 252), not quite reducible to it but, nevertheless, on certain conditions, convertible into it—forms that "produce their most specific effects only to the extent that they conceal (not least from their possessors) the fact that economic capital is . . . at the root of their effects" (p. 252). Furthermore, he described how the conservation of capital works precisely through conversions from one type of capital into another, and how symbolic conversions are marked by "the essential ambiguity of social exchange, which presupposes . . . a much more subtle economy of time" (p. 252).

For Bourdieu (1986), *capital* is power, social energy accumulated and appropriated as labor:

> Capital is accumulated labor (in its materialized form or its "incorporated," embodied form) which, when appropriated on a private, i. e., exclusive, basis by agents or groups of agents, enables them to appropriate social energy in the form of reified or living labor. (p. 241)

As material resources and internal powers of individuals, subject to appropriation and assimilation, exchanges and conversions, capital is a "force inscribed in objective or subjective structures" (Bourdieu, 1986, p. 241), a voucher, a password. Most importantly, it is a structuring force: The condition of *time* for acquisition and accumulation, the specific cumulative effect of *inertia* in reproduction, and the existence (at any given time) of unequally distributed and diverse *forms* of capital demarcate the possibilities of social practices. As he posited it:

> Capital, which in its objectified or embodied forms, takes time to accumulate and which, as a potential capacity to produce profits and to reproduce itself in identical or expanded form, contains a tendency to persist in its being, is a force inscribed in the objectivity of things so that everything is not equally possible or impossible. And the structure of the distribution of the different types and subtypes of capital at a given moment in time represents the immanent structure of the social world, i.e., the set of constraints, inscribed in the very reality of that world, which govern its functioning in a durable way, determining the chances of success for practices. (Bourdieu, 1986, pp. 241–242)

Therefore, he defined *symbolic capital* as "capital—in whatever form—insofar as it is represented, i.e., apprehended symbolically, in a relationship of knowledge or, more precisely, of misrecognition and recognition, [which] presupposes the intervention of the *habitus*, as a socially constituted cognitive capacity" (Bourdieu, 1986, p. 255), ergo education.

Cultural Capital

Cultural capital presents itself in three forms: (a) in the embodied state—its fundamental form—"as long-lasting dispositions of the mind and body;" (b) in the objectified state, as "cultural goods (pictures, books, dictionaries, instruments, machines, etc.), which are the trace or realization of theories or critiques of these theories;" and (c) in the institutionalized state, a distinctive form of objectification, as educational qualifications, that "confers entirely original properties on the cultural capital which it is presumed to guarantee" (Bourdieu, 1986, p. 243).

Embodied cultural capital is "external wealth converted into an integral part of the person, into a *habitus*" (Bourdieu, 1986, pp. 244–245), as exemplified by the learning required in order to play well a musical instrument, or by any intentionally developed competence. Therefore:

> ... it implies a labor of inculcation and assimilation, costs time, time which must be invested personally by the investor.... The work of acquisition is work on oneself (self-improvement), an effort that presupposes a personal cost ... an investment, above all of time, but also of that socially constituted form of libido, ... with all the privation, renunciation, and sacrifice that it may entail. (p. 244)

Cultural capital is also acquired "in the absence of any deliberate inculcation, and therefore quite unconsciously" (Bourdieu, 1986, p. 245), during the initial period of socialization: "The process of appropriating *objectified cultural capital* [italics added] and the time necessary for it to take place mainly depend on the cultural capital embodied in the whole family—through . . . [the automatic educative effect exerted by all cultural goods present in the child's environment, like books and computers] and all forms of implicit transmission" (p. 246), such as the images suggested by *parental involvement*. Thus, cultural capital "always remains marked by its earliest conditions of acquisition which, through the more or less visible marks they leave . . . , help to determine its distinctive value" (p. 245). This is the case of linguistic accents, social manners, dressing styles, tastes, and so forth, naturally acquired, without much of an effort, by immersion in social situations.

In class societies, where power asymmetries among social groups determine differentiated appropriation, as well as differentiated attribution of values for the available resources, and where access to the means of producing and enjoying cultural and material resources is uneven and an object of competition, scarcity generates profits of *distinction* for the owners of a large or highly valued form of cultural capital. The advantages secured by distinction are based, fundamentally, "on the fact that all agents do not have the economic and cultural means for prolonging their children's education beyond the minimum necessary for the reproduction of the labor-power least valorized at a given moment" (Bourdieu, 1986, p. 245). Thus, the very "structure of the field, i.e., the unequal distribution of capital, is the source of the specific effects of capital, i.e., the appropriation of profits and the power to impose the laws of functioning of the field most favorable to capital and its reproduction" (Bourdieu, 1986, p. 246). In the case of the structure of parental involvement, for instance, the uneven distribution of available parents across students' families, generates distinction (discernible in homework completion, and parental visibility in the school), and the likely agreement between teachers and involved parents about its benefits tends to legitimate and perpetuate it.

The time available for acquisition—"*time free from economic necessity*"— is, therefore, as Bourdieu (1986) made clear, what links economic and cultural capital:

> . . . the initial accumulation of cultural capital, the precondition for the fast, easy accumulation of every kind of useful cultural capital, starts at the outset, without delay, without wasted time, only for the offspring of families endowed with strong cultural capital; in this case, the accumulation period covers the whole period of socialization. It follows that the transmission of cultural capital is no doubt the best hidden form of hereditary transmission of capital, and it therefore receives proportionately greater weight in the system of reproduction strategies, as the direct, visible forms of transmission tend to be more strongly censored and controlled. (p. 246)

Furthermore, said Bourdieu (1986), because it is "linked in numerous ways to the person in his biological singularity and is subject to a hereditary transmission which is always heavily disguised, or even invisible," and "because the social conditions of its transmission and acquisition are more disguised than those of economic capital," *embodied cultural capital* tends to be "unrecognized as capital and recognized as legitimate competence" (p. 245), the result of innate talent or discrete, independent effort, conferring prestige or merit to its possessor.

Along this line, the properties of *objectified cultural capital,* "are defined only in the relationship with cultural capital in its embodied form" (Bourdieu, 1986, p. 246), for "the cultural object, as a living social institution, is, simultaneously, a socially instituted material object and a particular class of habitus, to which it is addressed" (p. 256). Thus, the specific appropriation of "the cultural capital objectified in material objects and media, such as writings, paintings, monuments, instruments, etc.," presupposes "the possession of the means of consuming" (pp. 246–247), that is, embodied capital. Nevertheless, "cultural capital in its objectified state presents itself with all the appearances of an autonomous, coherent universe . . . irreducible to that which each agent, or even the aggregate of the agents, can appropriate" (p. 247). Such appearance of autonomy is even greater in the case of *institutionalized cultural capital*:

> The objectification of cultural capital in the form of academic qualifications is one way of neutralizing some of the properties it derives from the fact that, being embodied, it has the same biological limits as its bearer. This objectification is what makes the difference between the capital of the autodidact, which may be called into question at any time, . . . and the cultural capital academically sanctioned by legally guaranteed qualifications, formally independent of the person of their bearer. With the academic qualification, a certificate of cultural competence which confers on its holder a conventional, constant, legally guaranteed value with respect to culture, social alchemy produces a form of cultural capital which has a relative autonomy vis-à-vis its bearer and even vis-à-vis the cultural capital he effectively possesses at a given moment in time. . . . In this case, one sees clearly the performative magic of the power of instituting, the power to show forth and secure belief or, in a word, to impose recognition. (Bourdieu, 1986, pp. 247–248)

By granting institutional recognition on the cultural capital held and manifested by individuals, *academic qualifications* are very instrumental:

> . . . the academic qualification makes it possible to compare qualification holders, . . . to establish conversion rates between cultural capital and economic capital by guaranteeing the monetary value of a given academic capital, . . . [and to establish] the value, in terms of cultural capital, of the holder of a given qualification relative to other qualification holders and, by the same token, the monetary value for which it can be exchanged on the labor market. (Bourdieu, 1986, p. 248)

Furthermore, the material and symbolic profits of academic qualifications are subject to scarcity, to fluctuation "in the conversion rate between academic capital and economic capital," and to uncertainty due to "changes in the structure of the chances of profit offered by the different types of capital" (Bourdieu, 1986, p. 248).

Social Capital

Social capital is defined by Bourdieu (1986) as resources derived from group membership:

> Social capital is the aggregate of the actual or *potential* resources which are linked to possession of a durable network of more or less institutionalized relationships of mutual acquaintance and recognition—or in other words, to membership in a group—which provides each of its members with the backing of the collectivity-owned capital, a "credential" which entitles them to credit, in the various senses of the word. (pp. 248–249)

Contrasting examples of such resources are the title of nobility—"the form *par excellence* of the institutionalized social capital which guarantees a particular form of social relationship in a lasting way" (Bourdieu, 1986, p. 251), and manners —"insofar as, through the mode of acquisition they point to, they indicate initial membership of a more or less prestigious group" (p. 256).

Coleman (1987) used a different concept of social capital as "the norms, the social networks, and the relationships between adults and children that are of value for the child's growing up" (p. 36). His notion of social capital as social values, resources, and patterns of interaction within intergenerational relationships in the family and community is not that of a symbolic currency linked to group membership, as in the case of Bourdieu's concept. Coleman seemed to focus on discrete structures that have educational value, whereas Bourdieu referred to structuring forces that create value or power within a complex and broad system of social exchanges.

According to Bourdieu (1986), social capital can be measured by "the size of the network of connections [a given agent] can effectively mobilize and . . . [by] the volume of the capital (economic, cultural or symbolic) possessed in his own right by each of those to whom he is connected (Bourdieu, 1986, p. 249). In this way, the reproduction of social capital requires continual endeavor of sociability, "which implies expenditure of time and energy and so, directly or indirectly, of economic capital" (Bourdieu, 1986, p. 250). On the one hand, such work requires specific competence:

> [It] . . . is not profitable or even conceivable unless one invests in it a specific competence (knowledge of genealogical relationships and of real connections and skill at using them, etc.) and an acquired disposition to acquire and maintain this competence, which are themselves integral parts of this capital. This is one of the factors which explain why the profitability of this labor of accumulating and maintaining social capital rises in proportion to the size of the capital. (Bourdieu, 1986, p. 250)

On the other hand, "the profits which accrue from membership in a group are the basis of the solidarity which makes them possible" (Bourdieu, 1986, p. 249):

> . . . the network of relationships is the product of investment strategies, individual or collective, consciously or unconsciously aimed at establishing or reproducing social relationships that are directly usable in the short or long term, i.e., at transforming contingent relations, such as those of neighborhood, the workplace, or even kinship, into relationships that are at once necessary and elective, implying durable obligations subjectively felt (feelings of gratitude, respect, friendship, etc.) or institutionally guaranteed (rights). (Bourdieu, 1986, pp. 249–250)

The constitution of meaningful social relationships is linked to the institution of occasions, places, and practices that control the legitimate forms of exchange and guarantee the homogeneity, boundaries, identity, and conditions of reproduction of a group. In turn, the individual–group dynamics related to concentration of social capital creates interesting effects of power, competition, and control through more or less institutionalized mechanisms of affiliation, delegation, and representation.

Thus, the concept of social capital and the images suggested by its active maintenance—and especially its profitable use in the context of the constitution of social groups and social identities (involving inclusion and exclusion), and increment of social resources and status—are interesting for the consideration of processes of group affiliation and social classification, as well as competition and individual achievement within selective institutions, such as schools. As Bourdieu (1986) pointed out:

> [The concept of social capital addresses] . . . the principle of social effects which, although they can be seen clearly at the level of singular agents— where statistical inquiry inevitably operates—*cannot be reduced to the set of properties individually possessed by a given agent* [italics added]. These effects . . . are particularly visible in all cases in which different individuals obtain very unequal profits from virtually equivalent (economic or cultural) capital, depending on the extent to which they can mobilize by proxy the capital of a group (a family, the alumni of an elite school, a select club, the aristocracy, etc.) that is more or less constituted as such and more or less rich in capital. (p. 256)

Conversions

The reproduction of capital (and, consequently, of social hierarchies) is effected through various strategies of conversion of its different types, albeit at the cost of some losses of capital. *Conversions* are understood as institutionalized mechanisms aimed at controlling and legitimating "the official, direct transmission of power and privileges" by disguising "the arbitrariness of the entitlements transmitted and of their transmission" (Bourdieu, 1986, p. 254).

It follows that "the different types of capital can be distinguished according to their reproducibility or, more precisely, according to how easily they are transmitted, i.e., with more or less loss and with more or less concealment" (Bourdieu, 1986, p. 253)—concealment and loss tending to correlate inversely. However, contradictorily, concealment of the "economic aspect also tends to increase the risk of loss (particularly the intergenerational transfers)" and, besides, "the (apparent) incommensurability of the different types of capital introduces a high degree of uncertainty into all transactions between holders of different types" (pp. 253–254). The transmission of cultural capital, for instance, as compared to economic capital, is subject to a more veiled but more risky transmission, as its "diffuse, continuous transmission within the family escapes observation and control," and as its "full efficacy, at least on the labor market," increasingly depends on validation by the educational system, i.e., on conversion into a "capital of qualifications" (p. 254).

Conversions, a form of indirect transmission, require time and specific work (including affective investment), according to the logic of minimization of both the work and losses inherent to the process. As capital is accumulated *labor-time*, so conversions also require labor-time to be effectively performed:

> In accordance with a principle which is the equivalent of the principle of the conservation of energy, profits in one area are necessarily paid for by costs in another.... The universal equivalent ... is nothing other than labor-time (in the widest sense); and the conservation of social energy through all its conversions is verified if, in each case, one takes into account both the labor-time accumulated in the form of capital and the labor-time needed to transform it from one type into another. (Bourdieu, 1986, p. 253)

Therefore, the "different types of capital can be derived from *economic capital*, but only at the cost of a more or less great effort of transformation, which is needed to produce the type of power effective in the field in question" (Bourdieu, 1986, p. 252). Such is the case of certain goods and services that are not immediately attainable through economic capital and impose secondary costs, particularly the cost of specific long-term previous investments—investments "not necessarily conceived as a calculated pursuit of gain," but likely to be "experienced in terms of the logic of emotional investment, i.e., as an involvement which is both necessary and disinterested" (p. 257). The conversion of economic capital into social capital, for instance, requires long-term investments in social relationships performed prior to their period of use:

> ... an apparently gratuitous expenditure of time, attention, care, concern, which ... has the effect of transfiguring the purely monetary import of the exchange [of a gift, service, visit] and, by the same token, the very meaning of the exchange. From a narrowly economic standpoint, this effort is bound to be seen as pure wastage, but in the terms of the logic of social exchanges, it is a solid investment, the profits of which will appear, in the long run, in monetary or other form" (Bourdieu, 1986, p. 253).

Similarly, the conversion of economic capital into cultural capital depends on the possession of economic capital, which enables and secures the expenditure of the time necessary for the transmission and acquisition of cultural capital:

> More precisely, it is because the cultural capital that is effectively transmitted within the family itself depends not only on the quantity of cultural capital, itself accumulated by spending time, that the domestic group possess, but also on the usable time (particularly in the form of the *mother's free time*) [italics added] available to it (by virtue of its economic capital, which enables it to purchase the time of others) to ensure the transmission of this capital and to delay entry into the labor market through prolonged schooling, a credit which pays off, if at all, only in the very long term. (Bourdieu, 1986, p. 253)

Moreover, the most precious gain secured by capital, and especially by cultural capital, "is the increased volume of *useful time* that is made possible through the various methods of appropriating other people's time" (Bourdieu, 1986, p. 258, italics added) by purchasing services and/or making one's own time more productive and profitable by applying to it especial knowledge and skills:

> It may take the form either of increased spare time, secured by reducing the time consumed in activities directly channeled toward producing the means of reproducing the existence of the domestic group, or of more intense use of the time so consumed, by recourse to other people's labor or to devices and methods which are available only to those who have spent time learning how to use them and which . . . make it possible to save time. (This is in contrast to the cash savings of the poor, which are paid for in time—do-it-yourself, bargain hunting, etc.) None of this is true of mere economic capital; *it is possession of cultural capital that makes it possible to derive greater profit not only from labor-time, by securing a higher yield from the same time, but also from spare time, and so to increase both economic and cultural capital.* (Bourdieu, 1986, p. 258, italics added)

Bourdieu (1986) also pointed out that, in our democratic era, "the more the official transmission of capital . . . [has been] prevented or hindered, the more the effects of the clandestine circulation of capital in the form of cultural capital [has] become determinant in the reproduction of the social structure" (p. 254), especially through conversion into academic capital. Consequently:

> As the educational qualification, invested with the specific force of the official, becomes the condition for legitimate access to a growing number of positions, particularly the dominant ones, the educational system tends increasingly to dispossess the domestic group of the monopoly of the transmission of power and privileges. (p. 254)

At the same time, the growth in objectified cultural capital available in the environment (which automatically increases its educative effect), combined with "the fact that embodied cultural capital is [also] constantly increasing," accounts for the fact that, "in each generation, the educational system can take more for granted" (Bourdieu, 1986, p. 256).

Nevertheless, Bourdieu (1986) stressed the relative power of the educational system in determining individual destinies—in terms of acquisition of academic capital (a diploma) convertible into economic and social capital (jobs and prestige):

> The direct transmission of economic capital remains one of the principal means of reproduction, and the effect of social capital ("a helping hand," "string-pulling," the "old boy network") tends to correct the effect of academic sanctions. Educational qualifications never function perfectly as currency. They are never entirely separable from their holders: their value rises in proportion to the value of their bearer, especially in the least rigid areas of the social structure. (p. 258)

Symbolic Violence

Education, for Bourdieu and Passeron (1977), is cultural reproduction: "the process through which a *cultural arbitrary* is historically reproduced . . . the equivalent, in the cultural order, of the transmission of genetic capital in the biological order" (p. 32, italics added). It is useful to recall, again, that *arbitrary* (in this case, a noun) means *based on judgment*, whose reason is not necessarily true or legitimate, and whose consequent (particular) *choice* is but one among other (in principle, possible) choices, a choice made possible in certain *conditions* by the act of a specific *power*. Based on this standpoint, Bourdieu and Passeron (1977) developed the following theses:

(1) "All *pedagogic action* is, objectively, symbolic violence insofar as it is the imposition of a cultural arbitrary by an arbitrary power" (p. 5).

(2) The "pedagogic action necessarily implies, as a social condition of its exercise, *pedagogic authority* and the *relative autonomy* of the agency commissioned to exercise it" (pp. 11–12).

(3) The pedagogic action necessitates a *pedagogic work* of formation of "a *habitus*, the product of internalization of the principles of a cultural arbitrary capable . . . of perpetuating [them] in practices" (p. 31).

(4) The *institutionalized educational system* derives its specific characteristics from its task of self-reproduction (production and reproduction of its conditions of existence), a task necessary for the realization of its essential function of cultural reproduction, that is, inculcation and reproduction of "a cultural arbitrary which it does not produce" (p. 54), a function that contributes to social reproduction.

By *symbolic violence* Bourdieu and Passeron (1977) refer to the exercise of "power which manages to impose meanings and to impose them as legitimate by concealing the power relations which are the basis of its force, [and by adding] . . . its own specific symbolic force to those power relations" (p. 4), therefore assuring their reproduction. The notion of symbolic violence is grounded on linked assumptions. First, that "any social formation . . . [is] a system of power relations and sense relations between groups or classes" (p. 5). Second, that symbolic relations are, simultaneously, relatively autonomous from and relatively dependent on power relations. Third, that symbolic forces or representations of legitimacy provide a specific (and specifically symbolic) contribution to the exercise and perpetuation of power.

Pedagogic Action

In this light, education—all *pedagogic action* (in any form, informal or institutionalized), or any relation of *pedagogic communication* – is "objectively, symbolic violence," as it consists of "the imposition and inculcation of a *cultural arbitrary* by an arbitrary mode of imposition and inculcation" (Bourdieu & Passeron, 1977, p. 6, italics added).

Pedagogic action is *objectively* symbolic violence in two senses. First, because its arbitrary power is based on tangible power relations, that is, the imposition and inculcation of a certain cultural arbitrary (among others) is based on concrete social conditions grounding the positions of the social groups or classes. Second, because the delimitation (selection and exclusion) of certain meanings "re-produces (in both senses) the arbitrary selection a group or class objectively makes in and through its cultural arbitrary" (Bourdieu & Passeron, 1977, p. 8). Thus, the cultural diversity that exists in a society is hierarchized according to the positions of power of the different groups, and that hierarchy is re-produced within institutionalized education through the privileged transmission of the dominant cultural arbitrary.

Within a system of more or less integrated, competing cultural arbitraries, and based on specific power relations among the social groups, a dominant form of pedagogic action emerges as "the one which most fully, though always indirectly, corresponds to the objective interests (material, symbolic and . . . pedagogic) of the dominant groups or classes, both by its mode of imposition [selection of methods and activities] and by its delimitation of what [selection of certain contents in detriment of others] and on whom [selection of apt individuals and exclusion of others] it imposes (Bourdieu & Passeron, 1977, p. 7).

In this way, the dominant system of education (the school, nowadays, in contrast with popular, family or ethnic education) "tends to secure a monopoly of legitimate symbolic violence" (Bourdieu & Passeron, 1977, p. 6), in order to reproduce not just the dominant culture but the position of dominance of a particular cultural arbitrary (e.g., philosophy, classic languages, and literature in the past, or mathematics, natural sciences, and computer technology in the present), contributing thereby to perpetuate a particular structure of domination.

Furthermore, the dominant pedagogic action and system of education mediates the interactions among the other (dominated) pedagogic actions and systems. As a result:

> . . . the system of pedagogic actions, insofar as it is subject to the effect of domination by the dominant pedagogic action, tends to reproduce, both in the dominant and in the dominated classes, misrecognition of the truth of the legitimate culture as the dominant cultural arbitrary, whose reproduction contributes towards reproducing the power relations. (Bourdieu & Passeron, 1977, p. 31)

Pedagogic Authority

Education presupposes *pedagogic authority*, "the basis of the sociological possibility of the pedagogic action" (Bourdieu & Passeron, 1977, p. 21):

> . . . a delegation of authority, which requires the pedagogic agency to reproduce the principles of the cultural arbitrary which a group or class imposes as worthy of reproduction both by its very existence and by the fact of delegating to an agency the authority needed in order to reproduce it. (p. 31)

Pedagogic authority is "automatically conferred on every pedagogic transmitter by the traditionally and institutionally guaranteed position he occupies in a relation of pedagogic communication" (Bourdieu & Passeron, 1977, p. 21). However, both the agency and agents may fall short of the task:

> The concept of pedagogic authority clearly has no normative content. . . . since the pedagogic authority has precisely the effect of ensuring the social value of the pedagogic action regardless of the 'intrinsic' value of the agency exerting it, and whatever, for example, the degree of technical or charismatic qualification of the transmitter. (p. 21)

Accordingly, "the pedagogic transmitters are from the outset designated as fit to transmit that which they transmit, hence entitled to impose its reception and test its inculcation by means of socially approved or guaranteed sanctions" (Bourdieu & Passeron, 1977, p. 20); and "the pedagogic receivers are disposed from the outset to recognize the legitimacy of the information transmitted and the pedagogic authority of the pedagogic transmitters, hence to receive and internalize the message" (p. 21). Moreover, because "the informational content of the message does not exhaust the content of the communication," and because "the sending of a message . . . always transmits at least the affirmation of the value of the pedagogic action, the pedagogic authority . . . always tends to eliminate the question of the informative efficiency of the communication" (p. 21).

Despite this, the agents objectively manifest, in their practice, misrecognition of the truth of pedagogic action as violence by inevitably representing its arbitrariness as *natural* and necessary, "along the lines of the primordial relation of pedagogic communication, i.e. the relationship between parents and children, or more generally, between generations" (Bourdieu & Passeron, 1977, p. 19)—a misrecognition that, while being the condition for its exercise, implies objective recognition of its legitimate authority, thus "reinforcing the arbitrary power which establishes it and which it conceals" (p. 13). Ultimately, the psychological mechanism of delegation of authority tends to produce in those who undergo the pedagogic action misrecognition of the objective truth of their culture as a cultural arbitrary, that is, *ethnocentrism.*

This contradiction, according to Bourdieu and Passeron (1977), is not solved by a *soft pedagogy,* for instance, nondirective methods, participation, and dialogue:

> The 'soft approach' may be the only effective way of exercising the power of symbolic violence in a determinate state of the power relations, and of variably tolerant dispositions towards the explicit, crude manifestation of arbitrariness.

> If some people are nowadays able to believe in the possibility of a pedagogic action without obligation or punishment, this is the effect of an ethnocentrism which induces them not to perceive as such the sanctions of the mode of imposition characteristic of our society. To overwhelm one's pupils with affection . . . is to gain possession of that subtle instrument of repression, the withdrawal of affection, a pedagogical technique which is no less arbitrary . . . than corporal punishment or disgrace. The objective truth of this type of pedagogic action is harder to perceive because, on the one hand, the techniques employed conceal the social significance of the pedagogic relation under the guise of a purely psychological relationship and, on the other hand, their place in the system of authority techniques making up the dominant mode of imposition helps to prevent agents formed by this mode of imposition from seeing their arbitrary character. (pp. 17–18)

However, "the delegation of the right of symbolic violence which establishes the pedagogic authority of a pedagogic agency is always a limited delegation" (Bourdieu & Passeron, 1977, p. 27). The autonomy of pedagogic agencies is limited, first of all, by "the social conditions for the exercise of a pedagogic action, i.e. cultural proximity between the cultural arbitrary imposed by that pedagogic action and the cultural arbitraries of the groups or classes subjected to it" (p. 25). Insofar as symbolic actions can only work to the extent that they encounter and reinforce *predispositions and interests,* "any action of symbolic violence which succeeds in imposing itself . . . objectively presupposes a [prior, virtual and tacit] delegation of authority" (p. 25), based on class–culture organic relations:

> The recognition a group or class objectively accords a pedagogic agency is always . . . a function of the degree to which the market value and symbolic value of its members depend on their transformation and consecration by that agency's pedagogic action. . . . in modern societies the middle classes, and more precisely those middle class fractions whose ascension most directly depends on the School, differ from the working classes by an *academic docility* [italics added] which is expressed in, among other things, their particular sensitivity to the symbolic effects of punishments or rewards and more precisely to the social-certification effect of academic qualifications. (Bourdieu & Passeron, 1977, pp. 27–28)

And the market, of course, functions as an additional limitation:

> In any given social formation, the sanctions, material or symbolic, positive
> or negative, juridically guaranteed or not, through which pedagogic authority
> is expressed, and which ensure, strengthen and lastingly consecrate the effect
> of a pedagogic action, are more likely to be recognized as legitimate . . . when
> they are applied to groups or classes for whom these sanctions are more
> likely to be confirmed by the sanctions of the market on which the economic
> and social value of the products of the different pedagogic actions is
> determined. (Bourdieu & Passeron, 1977, p. 27)

> [In effect,] . . . by unifying the market on which the value of the products of
> the different pedagogic actions is determined, bourgeois society . . . has
> multiplied the opportunities for subjecting the products of the dominated
> pedagogic actions to the evaluative criteria of the legitimate culture [ensuring
> the likelihood that a dominated cultural arbitrary and the cultural attainments
> of individuals from the dominated groups be devalued by the anonymous
> sanctions of the labour market, as well as by those of the cultural and
> academic markets], thereby affirming and confirming its dominance in the
> symbolic order. (Bourdieu & Passeron, 1977, p. 28)

For the many individuals who have been exposed to dominated pedagogic
actions, and who "are destined to discover that the cultural arbitrary whose worth
they have had to recognize in order to acquire it is worthless on an economic or
symbolic market dominated by the cultural arbitrary of the dominant classes"
(Bourdieu & Passeron, 1977, p. 29), what is left is blunt marginalization or the
conflicts of acculturation into the dominant culture.

In sum, the success of any pedagogic action is a function of "the system of
relations between the cultural arbitrary imposed by . . . [the dominant pedagogic
action] . . . and the cultural arbitrary inculcated by the earliest phase of upbringing
within the groups and classes from which those undergoing the pedagogic action
originate" (Bourdieu & Passeron, 1977, p. 30), implying various degrees of
recognition of the pedagogic authority of the pedagogic agency, and of mastery of
the code used in the pedagogic communication. Hence, the differential success of
the dominant pedagogic action among the receivers is a function of:

> (1) the *pedagogic ethos* proper to a group or class, i.e. the system of
> dispositions towards that pedagogic action and the agency [school] exerting
> it, defined as the product of the internalization of (a) the value which the
> dominant pedagogic action confers by its sanctions on the products of the
> different family pedagogic actions and (b) the value which, by their objective
> sanctions, the different social markets confer on the products of the dominant
> pedagogic action according to the group or class from which they come; and
> (2) *cultural capital*, i.e. the cultural goods transmitted by the different family
> pedagogic actions, whose value qua cultural capital varies with the distance
> between the cultural arbitrary imposed by the dominant pedagogic action

and the cultural arbitrary inculcated by the family pedagogic action within the different groups or classes. (Bourdieu & Passeron, 1977, p. 30)

Pedagogic work

Education also requires a continual and productive *pedagogic work*:

> . . . a process of inculcation which must last long enough to produce a durable training, i.e. a *habitus*, the product of internalization of the principles of a cultural arbitrary capable of perpetuating itself after the pedagogic action has ceased and thereby of perpetuating in practices the principles of the internalized arbitrary. (Bourdieu & Passeron, 1977, p. 31)

The productivity of the pedagogic work is measured by the degree to which the habitus is durable, transposable, that is, "capable of generating practices conforming with the principles of the inculcated arbitrary in a greater number of different fields" (Bourdieu & Passeron, 1977, p. 33), and exhaustive, that is, capable of completely reproducing those principles in the practices it generates. Hence, the accomplished form of the habitus depends on the degree of completion of the pedagogic work considered necessary and sufficient (in terms of legitimate content, mode, and length of inculcation) in order to produce the degree of cultural attainment and competence by which a group tends to recognize the successful individual. More specifically:

> . . . the degree of legitimate competence in legitimate culture by which not only the dominant but also the dominated classes tend to recognize the 'cultivated man' and against which the products of the dominated pedagogic actions, i.e. the different forms of the accomplished man as defined by the culture of the dominated groups of classes, come to be measured objectively. (Bourdieu & Passeron, 1977, p. 35)

As the object and effect of the pedagogic work, the concept of *habitus*— "the principle unifying and generating practices" (Bourdieu & Passeron, 1977, p. 34)—connects representations and practices, both in the individual and social realms. With respect to the individual, the habitus is a system of dispositions that "expresses, first, the *result of an organizing action*, with a meaning very close to that of words such as 'structure' . . . [and also] a manner of being, a habitual state (especially of the body), and, in particular, a *predisposition*, tendency, *propensity* or *inclination*" (pp. 67–68). As "a system of schemes of perception, thought, appreciation and action" (p. 35), the habitus contains "self-discipline and self-censorship (the more unconscious to the extent that their principles have been internalized)" (p. 40). With respect to the social group and individual–group relations, the habitus grounds personal and social identities, thus contributing "towards producing and reproducing the intellectual and moral integration of the group or class on whose behalf it is carried on" (p. 35). In this way, pedagogic work becomes a profitable substitute for external repression and, particularly, physical coercion (a sanction precisely to the failures of internalization of a cultural arbitrary):

> [It] . . . tends to produce a permanent disposition to give, in every situation . . . the right response (i.e. the one laid down by cultural arbitrariness, and no other) to symbolic stimuli emanating from the agencies invested with the pedagogic authority which has made possible the pedagogic work responsible for the habitus. (Bourdieu & Passeron, 1977, p. 36)

The more it is accomplished, then, the more the pedagogic work tends fully to produce "the objective conditions for misrecognition of cultural arbitrariness, i.e. the conditions for subjective experience of the cultural arbitrary as necessary" (Bourdieu & Passeron, 1977, p. 37), and for concealment of "the objective truth of the habitus as the internalization of the principles of a cultural arbitrary" (p. 39), consolidating group or class (ethical and logical) *ethnocentrism*.

Furthermore, because the function of pedagogic work is to keep order, it produces the discipline required by the order of the prevalent power relations:

> . . . by inculcation or exclusion, it tends to impose recognition of the legitimacy of the dominant culture on the members of the dominated groups or classes, and to make them internalize, to a variable extent, disciplines and censorships which best serve the material and symbolic interests of the dominant groups or classes when they take the form of self-discipline and self-censorship. (Bourdieu & Passeron, 1977, pp. 40–41)

And, consonant with "the dominant ideology of the legitimate culture as the only authentic culture, i.e. as universal culture" (Bourdieu & Passeron, 1977, p. 40), pedagogical work also tends to impose on the dominated groups "recognition of the illegitimacy of their own cultural arbitrary," for exclusion takes its "most symbolic force when it assumes the guise of self-exclusion" (pp. 41–42):

> . . . a dominant pedagogic action tends not so much to inculcate the information constituting the dominant culture (if only because pedagogic work has a lower specific productivity and a shorter duration when applied to groups or classes lower down the social scale) as to inculcate the fait accompli of the legitimacy of the dominant culture. It may do so by inducing those excluded from the ranks of the legitimate addressees . . . to internalize the legitimacy of their exclusion; by making those it relegates to second-order teaching recognize the inferiority of this teaching and its audience; or by inculcating, through submission to academic disciplines and adherence to cultural hierarchies, a transposable, generalized disposition with regard to social disciplines and hierarchies. (Bourdieu & Passeron, 1977, p. 41)

How does cultural reproduction, and individual–group inclusion and exclusion (as micro-processes, which continually reproduce the social classes), operate along the process of individual and interinstitutional education? It operates by means of successive, distinct habitus (primary and secondary, involving practical and symbolic levels of mastery), which are produced within and through diverse forms of pedagogic work (more or less traditional, implicit or explicit, involving practical or formal transferability of the habitus), in the biographical and intergenerational orders, across various educational agencies and contexts, and within the system of cultural dominance.

Because pedagogic work is an *irreversible process*, the primary habitus produced during the earliest phase of upbringing becomes "the basis for the subsequent formation of any other habitus" (Bourdieu & Passeron, 1977, p. 42). This means that the specific productivity of any secondary or subsequent pedagogic work is a function of the distance between the habitus it aims to inculcate and the habitus inculcated by primary or previous pedagogic work. From this perspective, any secondary pedagogic work, such as schoolwork, may be situated between maintenance or reinforcement (a mode aiming simply to confirm the primary habitus), and conversion (a mode aiming at the complete substitution of one habitus for another). On the one hand, the differential productivity of schooling fundamentally depends on early home education—"even and especially when the educational system denies this primacy in its ideology and practice"—for the practical dispositions acquired in everyday life learning, particularly through language acquisition, "more or less elaborated symbolically, depending on the group or class, predispose children unequally towards symbolic mastery of the operations implied" in the school curriculum (p. 43). But, on the other hand, it also depends on the extent to which the specific work of the school consolidates or denies (by deculturation and reculturation) the original habitus.

Because symbolic mastery (the explicitation of the principles at work in a practice, i.e., its theoretic codification) follows, logically and chronologically, the practical mastery of a practice, secondary mastery tends to profit from an early and close connection to practical mastery. Therefore, the success of the action of symbolic imposition depends on the degree to which pedagogic systematization meets the principles already held by the individual in a practical state—the *internal fit* yielded in learning. Yet, psychological theories have often ignored class–culture predicaments:

> Contrary to what is suggested by certain psychogenetic theories which describe intelligence development as a universal process of unilinear transformation of sensorimotor mastery into symbolic mastery, the respective primary work of the different groups or classes produces primary systems of dispositions which differ not merely as different degrees of explicitness of the same practice but also as so many types of practical mastery unequally predisposing their bearers to acquire the particular type of symbolic mastery that is privileged by the dominant cultural arbitrary. (Bourdieu & Passeron, 1977, pp. 49–50)

Along this line, any mode of inculcation producing a habitus can be situated between an implicit pedagogy (the unconscious inculcation of practical principles) and an explicit pedagogy (the methodical inculcation of articulated or formalized principles). While traditional modes of inculcation (defined as unconscious, *familiarizing* processes) rely mostly on direct, repeated expression (modeling) of "a habitus defined by practical transferability," secondary pedagogic work aimed at symbolic mastery is "objectively organized with a view to ensuring, by explicit inculcation of codified formal principles, the formal transferability of the habitus" (Bourdieu & Passeron, 1977, p. 48). Thus, in principle, the productivity of schooling (or any secondary pedagogic work) depends on the consideration of "the degree to which the addressees of the pedagogic message possess the code of the message," and on the creation of "the social conditions for communication by methodically organizing exercises designed to ensure accelerated assimilation of the code of transmission and, therefore, accelerated inculcation of the [specific] habitus" (p. 45). However, the more *traditional* (ergo, conservative) a mode of inculcation is, the more it tends to be "objectively organized by reference to a limited audience of legitimate addressees . . . equipped with the adequate [basic] habitus (i.e. the pedagogic ethos and cultural capital proper to the groups or classes whose cultural arbitrary it reproduces)" (p. 45).

In fact, the efficiency of modes of inculcation "cannot be defined independently of the content inculcated and the social functions which the pedagogic work in question fulfils in a determinate social formation" (Bourdieu & Passeron, 1977, p. 47). While "implicit pedagogy is doubtless the most efficient way of transmitting traditional, undifferentiated, 'total' knowledge," as in the case of apprenticeship, and while it certainly becomes ineffectual when applied to agents lacking prior attainment, it also "can be very 'profitable' for the dominant classes [in the context of a system of dominant–dominated pedagogic actions and cultural arbitraries] . . . by enabling the possessors of the prerequisite cultural capital to continue to monopolize that capital" (p. 47).

The implicitness and unspecificity of transmission is much more visible (by comparison) in the case of traditional societies, while less clear, but still actual, in modern schooling. The less delimited or autonomous the pedagogic work of the school in relation to that of the family is, the more schools can rely on an implicit pedagogy with respect to intellectual and social discipline, since the prerequisite work has been furthered at home (or, alternatively, in preschool). Along this line, we can understand the evolution represented by the introduction of explicit behavioral and instructional (including homework) contracts in current public school practice as an effort to formally implement a specific habitus that was taken for granted in homogeneous middle-class cultural contexts. We can also understand a variety of curricular and instructional reforms as attempts to maximize pedagogical efficiency, however, as general prescriptions, blind to their own arbitrary elements, as well as to the differentiated social conditions and individual habitus upon which they act. And reforms may be seen, conversely, as movements creating new realms of implicitness in instructional contents and methods in reaction to other movements toward explicitness, introduced when the mastery of the *rules of the game* by more individuals threatens or effectively diminishes the effect of the selective mechanisms of schooling related to its function of class reproduction via cultural reproduction. Will the substitution of portfolios for exams, for instance, yield more explicitness and fairness in learning and evaluation, from the perspective of class–culture inequalities? Are portfolios just a mechanism of enforcement of new intellectual attributes in the context of a new pedagogy, and immune to cultural background, or will they come to be a more efficient mechanism of selection of rarest attributes?

The important point here is the *specificity* of the pedagogic work of the school, that is, its content–method and its function–effect, in relation to different class–cultures. Thus, it is important to recall one fact:

> . . . the agents responsible for primary pedagogic work [home education] have themselves been very unequally prepared for symbolic mastery by secondary pedagogic work [their previous schooling] and are therefore very unequally capable of orienting primary pedagogic work towards the verbalization, formulation and conceptualization of practical mastery which are demanded by secondary pedagogic work [i.e., their children's schooling]. (Bourdieu & Passeron, 1977, p. 49)

In effect, primary pedagogic work "rests more completely on practical transferability the more rigorously the material conditions of existence subject . . . [a group] to the imperatives of practice, tending thereby to prevent the formation and development of the aptitude for symbolic mastery of practice" (Bourdieu & Passeron, 1977, p. 48). Conversely,

> . . . primary pedagogic work prepares that much better for secondary pedagogic work based on explicit pedagogy when exerted within a group or class whose material conditions of existence allow them to stand more completely aside from practice, in other words to 'neutralize' in imagination or reflection the vital urgencies which thrust a pragmatic disposition on the dominated classes. (Bourdieu & Passeron, 1977, p. 49)

> Thus, a practical mastery oriented towards the manipulation of things, with the correlative relation to words, is less favourable to theoretic mastery of the rules of literate verbalization [and classificatory conceptualization] than a practical mastery directed towards . . . the primacy of word manipulation. (Bourdieu & Passeron, 1977, p. 50)

However, *in the context of a dominant cultural arbitrary subordinating practical mastery to symbolic mastery of practices, schooling*—"the dominant pedagogic work which uses a traditional mode of inculcation" (Bourdieu & Passeron, 1977, p. 51)—*contradictorily fails to realize the very prerequisites of its specific productivity, tending to dispense with explicit inculcation of verbal practical mastery*, "the more completely practical mastery of the principles giving symbolic mastery has already been inculcated in the legitimate addressees by the primary pedagogic work of the dominant groups or classes" (p. 49):

It is precisely when its legitimate public is made up of individuals equipped by primary pedagogic work with a verbally-oriented practical mastery, that secondary pedagogic work which is mandated to inculcate above all the mastery of a language and of a relation to language can, paradoxically, content itself with an implicit pedagogy, especially as regards language, because it can count on a habitus containing, in practical form, the predisposition to use language in accordance with a literate relation to language. . . . Conversely, in secondary pedagogic work which has the declared function of inculcating practical mastery of manual techniques . . . the mere fact of using theoretic discourse to make explicit the principles of techniques of which working class children have practical mastery is sufficient to cast the knacks and tricks of the trade into the illegitimacy of makeshift approximation, just as 'general education' reduces their language to jargon, slang or gibberish. That is one of one the most potent effects of the theoretic discourse which sets an unbridgeable gulf between the holder of the principles (e.g. the engineer) and the mere practitioner (e.g. the technician). (Bourdieu & Passeron, 1977, p. 50)

Thus, the differential productivity of schooling according to ethnic group and social class is produced by the very exercise of its pedagogic work which, as described by Bourdieu and Passeron (1977), creates the following simultaneous effects: the delimitation of "its really possible addressees, excluding the different groups or classes more rapidly the more completely they lack the capital and ethos objectively presupposed by its mode of inculcation" (p. 51); the "misrecognition of the mechanisms of delimitation . . . [bringing about] recognition of its actual addressees as the legitimate addressees and of the length of the inculcation actually undergone by the different groups or classes as the legitimate length of inculcation" (p. 51); the legitimization of the mode of possession of cultural capital by the dominant classes expressed by "the cultivated relation to legitimate culture as a relation of familiarity" (p. 52); and the inculcation of "the ideology of the 'gift' as a negation of the social conditions of the production of cultivated dispositions" (p. 52). In short, insofar as it does not fully produce "the conditions for its own productivity, [the school] can fulfil its eliminatory function merely by default" (p. 51), concealing social exclusion "under the overt function of selection" (p. 52) within the set of its legitimate addressees, "thereby imposing more subtly the legitimacy of its products and hierarchies" (p. 51).

The history of modern education, according to Bourdieu and Passeron (1977), is the history of class cultural hegemony:

One of the least noticed effects of compulsory schooling is that it succeeds in obtaining from the dominated classes a recognition of legitimate knowledge and know-how (e.g. in law, medicine, technology, entertainment or art), entailing the devaluation of the knowledge and know-how they effectively command (e.g. customary law, home medicine, craft techniques, folk art and language . . .) and so providing a market for material and especially symbolic products of which the means of production (not least, higher education) are virtually monopolized by the dominant classes (e.g. clinical diagnosis, legal advice, the culture industry, etc.). (p. 42)

The Institutionalized Educational System

Finally, Bourdieu and Passeron explained how the dominant *institutionalized educational system* (the school) combines, within its structure and functioning, the (external) function of cultural reproduction to that of self-reproduction. So, on the one hand,

> . . . it produces and reproduces . . . the conditions for pedagogic work capable of reproducing . . . continuously, at the least expense and in regular batches, a habitus as homogeneous and durable as possible in as many as the legitimate addressees as possible (including the reproducers of the institution) . . . [and] conforming as closely as possible to the principles of the cultural arbitrary which it is mandated to reproduce. (Bourdieu & Passeron, 1977, pp. 56–57)

> [In other words,] . . . it produces and reproduces the necessary conditions for the exercise of its internal function of inculcating, which are at the same time the sufficient conditions for the fulfillment of its external function of reproducing the legitimate culture and for its correlative contribution towards reproducing the power relations. (Bourdieu & Passeron, 1977, p. 67)

As a condition for that, on the other hand, it also simultaneously reproduces itself as an institution, reproducing through time the institutional conditions for both the performance of its task and its own reproduction (including the production of its own agents), within the limits of its relative autonomy, that is, within "the limits laid down by an institution mandated to reproduce a cultural arbitrary and not to decree it" (Bourdieu & Passeron, 1977, p. 57). It is this tendency towards self-reproduction that explains "the cultural backwardness of school culture"—the fact that "the educational system tends to reproduce the changes occurring in the cultural arbitrary that it is mandated to reproduce only after a time-lag commensurate with its relative autonomy" (p. 61).

Institutionalization, meaning autonomization through delegation, implies a series of interrelated features. It employs "a permanent corps of specialized agents [imbued with the *ideology of disinterestedness* and] equipped with the homogeneous training and standardized, standardizing instruments which are the precondition for the exercise of a specific, regulated process of pedagogic work" (Bourdieu & Passeron, 1977, p. 57). It imposes homogeneity, orthodoxy, and routinization of the work, insofar as the institutional demands related to the reproduction of the conditions for the continual exercise of the pedagogic work (whatever the habitus to be inculcated, and whatever the field), along with "the tendencies inherent in a corps of agents [themselves as little irreplaceable as possible] placed in these institutional conditions" (pp. 58–59), tend to subject information and training (the school message) to codification, standardization and systematization, "both dispensing and preventing the agents from performing heterogeneous or heterodox work" (p. 57). It "monopolizes the production of the agents appointed to reproduce it, i.e. of the agents equipped with the durable training which enables them to perform the work of schooling tending to reproduce the same training in new reproducers" (p. 60). It establishes school authority, that is, it provides the specific means of inhibiting and invalidating the possibility of the question of the legitimacy of the school action (its entitlement with respect to contents and methods of education), by producing and reproducing, "by the means proper to the institution, the institutional conditions for misrecognition of the symbolic violence which it exerts, i.e. recognition of its legitimacy as a pedagogic institution" (p. 61):

> [Through school authority,] . . . reproducing within the institution the delegation of authority from which the institution benefits, the educational system produces and reproduces the conditions necessary both for the exercise of an institutionalized pedagogic action and for the fulfillment of its external function of reproduction, since institutional legitimacy dispenses the agents of the institution from having endlessly to win and confirm their pedagogic authority. (Bourdieu & Passeron, 1977, p. 63).

However, school authority can be doubted, as exemplified by cases of indiscipline and school violence:

> . . . at moments of crisis when the tacit contract of delegation legitimating the educational system is threatened, the teachers . . . are called upon to resolve, each on his own behalf, the questions which the institution tended to exclude by its very functioning. The objective truth of the teacher's job, i.e. the social and institutional conditions which make it possible (pedagogic authority), is never more clearly revealed than when the crisis of the institution makes the job difficult or impossible. (Bourdieu & Passeron, 1977, p. 62)

The ultimate effect of institutionalization, which Bourdieu and Passeron (1977) called "dependence through independence," is the misrecognition, by those who exercise the schoolwork and those who undergo it, of "its dependence on the power relations making up the social formation in which it is carried on." As "the institutional means available to it as a relatively autonomous institution monopolizing the legitimate use of symbolic violence are predisposed to serve additionally, hence under the guise of neutrality, the groups or classes whose cultural arbitrary it reproduces," the dominant educational system, "by the mere fact of existing and persisting as an institution . . . implies the institutional conditions for misrecognition of the symbolic violence it exerts" (p. 67).

Possibilities and Limits of Educational Change

Those of us who work in and for schooling (teachers, policymakers, and researchers, who have bought thus far into the system as to become its professionals) wish to make it work well *for all students*, according to the old strain. The crucial issue in educational policy and practice has been how to guarantee more and better learning (to increase school productivity), distributing formal education more evenly across differentiated social groups and individuals (equalizing outcomes) so that its material and symbolic benefits can be democratized. Yet, given the very limits of our own cultural arbitrary as successfully schooled people, and the fact that we are functionaries of the system working within its logic, our individual actions are limited in range. As researchers and policymakers we tend to generalize partial or ideal situations, as basic assumptions and/or goals. As teachers we try to listen to our students (though their speech is constrained from the start by the curriculum and by our authority), and share with them our knowledge and experiences as learners and our commitments as educators (though our role embraces our own distinct interests), while trying to be fair in grading them. Moreover, beyond the amplitude of our efforts is the underlying issue of what knowledge and culture have constituted and should constitute formal education, as learning depends on the meaning and usefulness of the content prescribed.

According to Bourdieu and Passeron (1977), two solutions have been tried regarding the democratization of schooling: "the 'culture for the masses' programme of 'liberating' the dominated classes by giving them the means of appropriating legitimate culture as such, with all it owes to its functions of distinction and legitimation" (pp. 23–24); and "the populist project of decreeing the legitimacy of the cultural arbitrary of the dominated classes as constituted in and by the fact of its dominated position, canonizing it as 'popular culture'" (p. 24). However, as they said, both these solutions disregard the implications of the system of dominant–dominated cultural arbitraries, precisely what both "the legitimate culture and the dominated culture owe to the structure of their symbolic relations, i.e. to the structure of the relation of domination between the classes" (p. 23), and, ultimately, the fact that fluctuations in the value of the kinds of cultural capital are determined by the economic market.

The traditional solution comes down to making the school promise true by realizing its proper pedagogic function: The transmission of valued academic knowledge consonant with the dominant cultural arbitrary, or the teaching and learning of the language of power, as Delpit (1988) put it, which may function both as capital and as a means of self-fulfillment. It has been carried all along the history of schooling by devoted teachers and translated into various compensatory education and effective school programs. Yet, this solution usually focuses on change of instructional strategies and methods. Moreover, insofar as the ample accomplishment of the pedagogic function is logically seen as precisely counteracting the customary selective function of schooling, the low or uneven productivity of the school cannot really be explained within this model, except in terms of teachers' or students' shortcomings, such as lack of commitment or motivation.

The alternative (minor) solution has been the so-called *multicultural curriculum*, through which the dominant cultural arbitrary is apparently altered in order to fit other world views, which might be interpreted as an attempt to unbalance the cultural relations of power by redefining cultural capital. Nevertheless, the addition of diverse cultural perspectives might just create a *potpourri curriculum* without changing other aspects of the traditional structure of authority and work of the school, particularly the conception and practice of assessment. To complicate matters, it is not clear what the market value of alternative curricula could be.

In contemplating the hypothesis of democratization of education (i.e., legitimate culture), Bourdieu and Passeron (1977) examined whether a type of secondary pedagogic work "organized in accordance with the principles of an explicit pedagogy, would not have the effect of erasing the boundary which traditional pedagogic work recognizes and confirms between the legitimate addressees and the rest" (p. 53). More precisely:

> . . . whether perfectly rational pedagogic work . . . taking nothing for granted at the outset, with the explicit goal of explicitly inculcating in all its pupils the practical principles of the symbolic mastery of practices which are inculcated by primary pedagogic action only within certain groups or classes . . . would not correspond to the pedagogic interest of the dominated classes. (p. 53)

In other words, if school effectively taught the language of power to all and especially those students particularly deprived of it, would its discriminatory function disappear, and would the so-called deprived students recognize the necessity and (perhaps strategic) value of the dominant culture?

Their answer raises two problems. First, they pointed out the utopian character of educational policy aimed at democratization insofar as "the structure of power relations prohibits a dominant pedagogic action from resorting to a type of pedagogic work contrary to the interests of the dominant classes who delegate its pedagogic authority to it" (Bourdieu & Passeron, 1977, pp. 53–54). Indeed, solutions like compensatory education or critical–liberatory pedagogy (teaching explicitly and effectively the language and skills of power, and the workings of the system) have always been known and attempted in a small scale. The very fact that they have not been generally implemented, albeit technically and financially possible, explains why they will not be easily and largely implemented. Second, they cautioned against the mistake of identifying the objective interests of the dominated classes with the individual interests of some of their members (who have advanced by mastering the language and skills of power), insofar as "the controlled mobility of a limited number of individuals can help to perpetuate the structure of class relations" (p. 54).

If the public school historically appeared as an instrument of upward social mobility and class hegemony (the ascension of the bourgeoisie), how can it promote equality? Equalization of access under the imposition of one cultural arbitrary (and the consequent devaluation of other cultural arbitraries) necessarily creates inequality of outcomes, as explained by the theory of symbolic violence (Bourdieu & Passeron, 1977). Solutions like curricular differentiation (tracking) apparently democratize by allowing longer permanence and increase of high school graduation, albeit skirting the cultural capital issue. The compensatory education approach surely requires that the students who lack the valued cultural capital pay a much higher price to succeed in school by acculturation. However, the possibility of equalization would remain narrow insofar as, due to different starting points and due to the property of accumulation, some individuals would always hold more cultural capital than others, and due to investment of other forms of social and economic capital and their combined influence, some individuals would still have more of an advantage than others. In short, within the dominant cultural arbitrary of capitalist schooling, equality is antithetic to meritocracy, which justifies the limits of upward social mobility within the educational system.

Furthermore, even if schools produced equality (equally enlightened and competent individuals, holders of equally high credentials) social and economic inequality would not necessarily disappear as a consequence. For one reason, despite the common contrary belief, social and economic inequality is more a cause than an effect of educational outcomes. For another reason, educational attainment does not automatically turn into jobs and salaries; complex market mechanisms and the play of social capital mediate between educational credentials, occupational positions, and socioeconomic rewards. The relative autonomy of schooling in front of the social–economic realm precisely implies that, on the one hand, school does not automatically reproduce but, rather, *converts* social inequalities; and, yet, on the other hand, it cannot directly determine but, rather, *reproduces* social and economic relations.

EDUCATIONAL POLICY, EQUITY, AND THE FAMILY

The end of the 19th century saw a peak in enthusiasm for education. At the end of 20th century, the information available about the doubtful accomplishments of an era of schooling in regard to social equalization offered no reason to be enthusiastic. Nor were there new educational promises in the air. To be sure, the current discourse on education is not about social justice and personal happiness but about economic competitiveness, school efficiency, and individual success. Within the framework of globalization, and consonant with the neo-liberal surge, intense demands are posed: the social efficiency goal of schooling has been renewed through expanded attention to test scores (and international grade-performance comparisons), stress on student accountability, new impetus at curricular centralization, school finance reforms with incentives for downsizing and cost optimization, simultaneous emphasis on computers and "the basics," and the assignment to the family of the job of securing school accountability through the school choice movement.

Interestingly, we saw in this last decade of the 20th century a nostalgia for old forms and meanings of education, family, and community. A most startling point is the return to home or family education, either through grassroots initiatives, like the home schooling movement, or through the official recognition of "families as educators" by both the educational research and policy establishments (e.g.,

Coleman, 1991; AERA's Families as Educators Special Interest Group). Whereas research has focused on family educational workings and parenting styles conducive (or not) to school success, and suggested how schools can help families in order that families help the schools to educate their children (Henderson & Berla, 1995), policy has been advancing a *necessary* shift from the *delegation model* to the *partnership model* (Seeley, 1993) in family–school relations.

The hopes now are not deposited on the school but, instead, on the family. And again, the voices in the research and policy communities dealing with the articulation of schools and families speak from the grounds of the traditional middle-class family, or the latest case of successful immigrant family (currently Southeast-Asian) who employed the "right" attitudes and values (Caplan, Choy, & Whitmore, 1992). In this context, Bourdieu and Passeron's theoretical model offers a much needed perspective by connecting the processes of social reproduction (physical, emotional, and cognitive) initiated in the home environment to the function of symbolic violence (as a strategy of cultural and social class reproduction) carried by compulsory schooling, with its shameless processes of selection based on family cultural capital. It allows us to understand precisely why and delimit under what sociocultural conditions families have been important for school success, and precisely why and under what pedagogical conditions schools have implemented cultural discrimination and reproduced social inequalities.

To recapitulate, schools implement social reproduction fundamentally through the reproduction of the dominant cultural arbitrary, that is, through the dissemination and conservation of a particular form of knowledge (and consequent condemnation of various knowledges to illegitimacy and oblivion), and secondarily through the reproduction of social hierarchies, that is, by sorting students according to their possession of the "right" knowledge. By specifically building on family-class diverse cultures, the school action may vary from merely confirming social hierarchies by validating the "right" *habitus*—in which case it combines a great reliance on the family, with an implicit pedagogy with a major accent on assessment; to providing effective opportunities for the acquisition of academic culture—in which case it realizes the specificity of its pedagogic work by developing an explicit pedagogy with a greater stress on teaching and learning. Of course, the greater the stress on family educational accountability, the tighter cultural imposition and selection, and, consequently, the likeliness of inequity. Without *cultural translation,* within a context of respect for diverse cultures, the meaning of educational opportunity cannot be fulfilled.

It could be argued that Bourdieu and Passeron's theory is too pessimistic and that, in allowing for no hope, it would discourage efforts toward equity in schooling. I counter that accounting for the tendency toward social reproduction, that is, for the narrow range of possibility of sociostructural transformation, is indispensable for counteracting intelligently and effectively the inertia of traditional practices, as well as for reading the reproductivist aspects of novel practices. It is useful to recall that social reproduction is indispensable, yet awareness of what is reproduced, at what cost, and for the benefit of whom, is important.

Knowing what is known about the reproduction of social inequality within schooling, a fascinating question at this point is: Why is the family now being called to exert a crucial educational role and an urgent contribution to successful schooling? What are, then, the good reasons why schools should abandon the traditional delegation model and enforce the so-called new partnership model? In order to explore this movement, and to close this analysis around the questions of fairness and viability of parental involvement as a policy, I take four lines of thought. First, concerning the family, I caution against its definition as an educational institution and against educational policy defining home education as an aid to schooling. Second, I argue that while the meaning of the public school is currently at stake, the policy emphasis on the family as educator, implying formal family accountability, is not auspicious nor viable for many families, due to material and symbolic factors. Third, I alert that, insofar as *parenting* functions as symbolic capital, and teachers expect a certain ostensibly supportive parental role, parental involvement creates a context in which teachers are likely to discriminate among students based on their parents' performance. And, finally, I spell out some of the contradictions of the parental involvement model, and what a policy concerned with equity would pose in terms of school goals and family–school relations.

The Family Is Not an Educational Institution

By making this point, of course, I do not intend to deny that all families educate, but rather to affirm that formal education or instruction is not (and never really was) the foremost or special function of families. If this is so, and if, moreover, the nuclear family is a construction of the modern state, having been historically dependent (including pioneer and suburban families) on public support, as Coontz (1992) averred, it is very curious that the family is being rhetorically redefined as an educational institution at the very moment in which it is suffering a quite marked and costly transformation.

Coleman (1987) pointed out that "families at all economic levels are becoming increasingly ill-equipped to provide the setting that schools are designed to complement and augment in preparing the next generation" (p. 32). Growth in single-parent and two-earner households, and also in poverty of families with children due to "increasing distribution of income away from households that have children or other dependents" (p. 33), has paralleled the contraction of the welfare state. According to Sanders (1995), *The Chicago Tribune* reported, not long ago:

> As of 1992, 10.1 million families in America were headed by a single parent, usually the mother. This works out to be about one-third of all families with children in this country, and represents a 300 percent increase since 1970. Demographers predict that by the turn of the century, half the children in this country will grow up in single-parent families. (p. 186)

Although unemployment is said to be low at the beginning of the 21th century, work conditions seem to have deteriorated for some occupations, with the expansion of jobs by-the-hour, rotating shifts, and sweat shops (employing the new immigrant) that resemble the early times of industrialization. Even those who can survive decently feel constantly pressed by all the needs and obligations created by the organization of a consumerist society, which dictates aspirations and lifestyles, and overall has made free time a rare good available only to the very rich. As a result, working parents do not dispose of quality time either for themselves or for their children. According to Fuchs, Sanders (1995) stated that:

> ... the amount of time parents have to spend with their children has decreased about 40 percent since World War II. Between 1960 and 1986, the potential time with parents for white children dropped by ten hours a week, and by twelve hours for black children due to increases in mothers' employment, in fathers' increased working hours, and in the incidence of single-parent households. (p. 191)

Thus, the emphasis on parenting runs contradictorily to these trends.

Within the macro-historical picture, the appeal of the current call on the family can be traced to its remote cultural origin in the "school-as-an-extension-of-the-family" middle-class model—still actual, to a limited extent—that is historically (individually and institutionally) the model of successful schooling. Coleman (1987) described the traditional family–school partnership in the following way: formal institutions of child rearing are structured to provide for "a certain class of inputs into the socialization process . . . characterized as *opportunities, demands,* and *rewards,*" while the family ("the child's closer, more intimate, and more persisting environment") is supposed to impart "a second class of inputs . . . described as *attitudes, effort,* and *conception of self*" (p. 35).

There is more, however, to this second class of inputs than Coleman's choice of terms might suggest: The primary *habitus*, according to Bourdieu and Passeron (1977), really renders the basic psychological, and specifically cognitive structure, as well as cultural, and specifically linguistic structure, which, in conditions of cultural continuity, productively interact with the social, specifically pedagogic, stimuli of the school. And it is also crucial to note that the educational character of the family has basically lain in the full-time dedication of the mother, and that the typical homemaker, in this case, has been educated herself. In effect, the traditional (successful) family–school partnership has counted on "the best hidden and socially most determinant educational investment, namely, the domestic transmission of cultural capital" (Bourdieu, 1987, p. 243), based on the mother's time, embodied cultural capital, and available social capital.

Thus, the call on the family as educator is consistent with the pedagogic ethos of the schooled middle classes, and eventually with the upward mobility project of some low-class families and social groups (including immigrant), in that it merely confirms their lifestyle and aspirations. Insofar as the policy of parental involvement consecrates the traditional practices of some families, these very families are getting a formal insurance while continuing to help their kids take advantage of educational opportunities. For other families, the policy might function as an incentive: It is likely that a few low class families will again benefit (as in the past, especially when supported by effective programs) and attest the lack of interest and effort of the majority of losers, repeating the old strain. However, a majority of families cannot fit the partnership model, as they have not inherited and are not likely to produce (due to their concrete life conditions) the cultural and social forms of capital likely to work as currency in their exchanges with the school.

It is also curious, from a historical perspective, to find that the current emphasis on family educational responsibility runs counter to the ideology of the superiority of public schooling over home and community education, which justified compulsory schooling in terms of political purposes and socioeconomic viability. In fact, consideration of family diversity, especially regarding social class and meanings of schooling for different social groups, reveals the inaccuracy of the notion that modern schooling substituted and supplanted the family in education, under the new urban-industrial conditions of social reproduction.

First, the school could have substituted only those families that were in a condition of offering literate education, which in turn did not need the public school, having mostly preferred to rely on private arrangements. Schools—and the public school, especially—are dispensable for the reproduction and transmission of economic capital of the wealthy, as discrete families, but of course not as the dominant class, due to the ideological function of schooling in sustaining the dominant culture. For the reproduction of cultural capital, specifically the sophisticated canons of the dominant cultural arbitrary, and also for the concentration of social capital, the wealthy have relied on exclusive private schools.

Second, the modern school came to offer exactly what poor, peasant, urban and immigrant families lacked: lettered education, national identity and industrial discipline, the path to sociocultural and economic integration and perhaps, social mobility. However, a division of reproductive and educative work between family and school (functional differentiation) was concretely constructed: Their roles and tasks in the care and instruction of children became specialized, moreover tending to be exclusive, albeit articulated and complementary. This exclusivity is based on separate spaces and times of school and family lives, as well as on distinct practices, to say the least. A banal indicator is the fact that both teachers and parents perceive the specificity and exclusivity of their tasks and are eager to defend their prerogatives. Regarding parents, one example is the current "parental and family rights" movement. Teachers, in turn, despite contrary rhetoric, do not welcome parental interference in the classroom, as some researchers have pointed out (e.g., Biklen, 1995; Dornbusch & Ritter, 1988).

Traditionally, in varying degrees, schools and teachers have seen the role of families and parents as one of preparing for (particularly in preschool and elementary school years), supporting, and reinforcing academic work on a daily basis, especially when students present difficulties. Besides home backing, teachers and principals also expect parents to participate in a variety of school social activities—sports, parties, fund-raising, and some limited level of decision making in school governance—all prone to lend symbolic support. Some families and parents, specifically academically oriented middle-class, and occasionally those from lower class and minority groups struggling for social mobility, have assumed such in-home and/or in-school supportive roles. The positive participation of parents within the framework aforementioned—positive in the sense of not creating conflicts, but rather helping to solve problems according to the school's orientation—has reinforced the model of parental involvement expected by teachers and now promoted by educational policy.

However, when schools and teachers expect parental involvement both in school and with homework, they do not consider the cases of single parents, working mothers, ethnic and language minority families, low-educated, handicapped, and chronically ill parents, those with a great number of children, in poverty, as well as those working irregular, night, and double shifts—all of whom have time constraints and limited skills and resources, and who add up to the majority of parents of public schools. It is reasonable that parents in these difficult life situations, feeling that they already make great sacrifices in order to feed, keep healthy, and bring their children to school, expect the school to provide for precisely that which they cannot afford at home or with their own resources, and at a minimum cost for them. It does not seem reasonable nor efficient, on the other hand, to expect schools and teachers to *help* these kinds of parents and their children through additional academic work, creating an extra function for the school (social assistance and adult education), an extra burden for teachers (social worker and parent educator), and the possibility of blaming parents for their irresponsiveness.

Because the material, cultural, and personal conditions of families are not evenly available to perform an educational role influential on school success, how can one make sense of the subliminal—and, now, quite explicit—charge at parental accountability within the formalization of the family–school partnership? Whereas within the dominant cultural arbitrary of schooling, the typical partnership in which parents support the school curriculum makes total sense and is not perceived as an imposition (because there is identity and continuity of values and practices among middle-class parents and education professionals), this is certainly not the case for the majority of lower class and cultural minority parents. Nevertheless, insofar as the educational workings of the family are subordinated to the school (where home education is confirmed or denied), by framing the family as an educational institution—not quite in its own right, but designated with the obligation of providing the basic inputs for the development of the school curriculum—educational policy can, in fact, not only legitimately fail those students whose parents do not comply with their educational obligation to their children, but rightfully dictate family education.

This contradiction has already generated reactions of some families and groups. The home-schoolers, for instance, are attempting to do education in their own right and by their own means, withdrawing taxes from public education. The so-called religious right groups, in turn, who charge the public (state) school with totalitarianism (e.g., Luksik & Hoffecker, 1995), are the more likely to resent conflicts between school and family cultures, the more the school curriculum penetrates the home. Yet, this contradiction is not likely to be easily worked out by the many families who lack the resources, the time, and the voice to intervene politically in the realm of public education.

The Purposes and Meanings of the Public School

The public school appeared as a solution for the intellectual education of a small collectivity, resembling what is called a private school today. The meaning of public, as we came to understand it, is connected to the advent of the state compulsory school, which represented a greater collectivity and supposed a common knowledge, a special purpose, and a unique context of experience, which could not be accomplished by any other form of education or social institution, as purported by the ideology of modern democratic schooling. So, modern education is precisely epitomized by the public, secular school, open to all citizens, whose mission, although intellectual, is social, and although political, is collective bound.

On the one hand, in contrast with the fact that schooling became its predominant mode, the very idea that public education is a joint responsibility of the state, families, and communities presupposes diversity and specialization, differentiated powers and responsibilities, within a framework of convergent purposes, that is, a conception of public interest. Historically, as the work community declined, the new *social contract* of education and social reproduction split personal and common, affective and cognitive aspects between the nuclear family and the school: Psychosocial and moral development remained primarily as the camp of the family, while the specific task of the school was defined as intellectual and collective-moral development. On the other hand, within this social contract, public education has been assigned two main purposes: democratic construction (citizenship education), and social efficiency (labor training), the second being subordinated to the first, at least rhetorically. Fundamentally, democratic construction presupposes not only formal and actual equality of educational opportunity (so that individuals can have equal chances of developing their skills and competing for positions of power in order to serve the collectivity), but a common experience and knowledge that result in a minimum set of shared values and social solidarity.

However, as schooling evolved, it offered diverse experiences and embodied distinct meanings for different social classes, groups, and individuals, depending basically on their relation to literate culture and on the place they occupied—and could come to occupy, depending on the movements of the market—in the relations of production. While wealthy families never needed the public school, the middle classes have been quite successful in privatizing it, that is, in shaping the educational service offered by their neighborhood school, through active involvement and subtle pressures to get a tailored education for their children, as Lareau (1987, 1993) demonstrated. For working-class individuals, the public school represented a kind of education quite distinct from their home background, and the only opportunity of access to formal education and, eventually, white-collar jobs, whereas for the underclass it did not mean any hope. As a result, academic knowledge (represented by a credential), which is a condition for social opportunity in the present mode of social reproduction, has not been accessible to all, and has been disproportionately denied to the lower classes. From a cultural perspective—in the conditions of imposition of a particular cultural arbitrary on all, of traditional cultural wars, and of unstableness of academic knowledge—it seems fair to say that the common knowledge necessary for democratic construction and solidarity has been hardly developed and precariously realized.

Diverse school experiences and outcomes related to distinct social class cultures originated two models of family–school relations: the partnership model of the middle classes, and the delegation model of the lower classes, tempered by various degrees of resistance to the school culture (Connell, Ashenden, Kessler, & Downsett, 1982). Notwithstanding, the current policy rationale on the necessity and benefit of parental involvement, based on the "school-as-an-extension-of-the-family" model, carries a typical middle-class bias in that it assumes the intrinsic value of education for self-accomplishment, and/or the ideology of education for upward social mobility, counting on the fiction that all parents value academic education, desire school success, believe it is conducive to social power and economic affluence, and are able to invest in it.

Meanings of education and schooling are produced by concrete life conditions and school experiences. Parents' expectations and investments toward their children's schooling, and particularly their contributions to learning, depend on various intertwined factors:

- generally, on material and cultural resources (the later being dependent on the former to a greater extent), on their social class framework (work and life style), on the extent in which they have bought into the promises of the liberal ideology (individualism, competition, and pursuit of advantage), and on some sort of more or less conscious calculation of costs and benefits, considering all of the other life needs, circumstances and challenges;
- specifically, on their own *habitus* and school experience, that is, on the extent to which they have been successfully schooled and acquainted with erudite culture themselves;
- and, last but not least, on children's (individually differentiated) school performance that, being a source of gratification or frustration for parents, interacts with the above general and specific factors.

On a very practical level, granted that they share the dominant cultural arbitrary, parents' involvement in education requires, minimally, free time and money to enjoy and introduce children into literate culture: time to be with children after work and after all the other tasks of daily life reproduction have been taken care; and money to pay for a baby-sitter in order to attend a school meeting, to buy a ready meal instead of cooking in order to help with homework. On the symbolic level, the meanings parents assign to school knowledge, experiences, and credentials are related in complex ways to family history, current life situation, and aspirations.

Yet, specific engagement in instruction depends not only on parents' own academic background and mastery of subject matters, but on their keeping up with successive curricular reforms, and thus on a especial interest in schooling.

Traditionally, middle-class families have taken advantage of educational opportunities. Independently from school explicit policy, middle-class parents are known for getting actively involved in school and promoting academic culture at home. Their motivations are various, but basically they strive to stimulate their children to learn the school curriculum and succeed, assuring them of the value of education and individual effort, bolstering their self-esteem and compensating for frustrations. They may participate in school activities as a way to show their children how much they value education and, thus, reinforce expectations of school success. They may show up at school as a kind of insurance regarding future needs, thus increasing the chances that their kids will profit from positive discrimination by being related to concerned parents, or as a strategy to influence specific school policies and practices for their advantage. They may join extracurricular activities that offer opportunities to socialize and meet friends for their own leisure purposes, as in the case of sports and arts. They may follow the academic curriculum at school (by volunteering in the classroom) or at home, either because they value it and try to reinforce it, or object to it and try to modify it, or else because of their students' especial needs. They may engage more or less in homework according to students' peculiarities, such as talent, difficulty, or dependency, or because they want to compensate for curricular weaknesses independently, at home. The very model of loving parents, according to the middle-class cultural arbitrary, includes a concern with children's academic, social and economic success.

While a variety of forms of family–school partnership have worked for the middle classes, poor and working-class families have had to delegate schooling to the state, the school, and the teacher, for complex material and cultural reasons. Beyond material constraints, the association between education and personal enjoyment and success is not part of their concrete experience or a promise of their cultural arbitrary, and they lack the very educational prerequisites to get involved in schooling. Insofar as those parents were not educated when they were younger, it is all the more unfair to expect them to invest in their own education as working adults (return to school or attend parenting workshops) in order to educate their children, when their life circumstances are very different and harder than those of the middle and upper classes. Consequently, it is not only unjust to call lower class parents passive, but it also seems untenable to expect their participation to increase on the basis of a policy call and teacher leadership, as pretended by Epstein (1991). Insofar as conditions of life and meanings of education are doomed to persist differentiated for the various social groups, school's reliance on the family is generally implausible.

In this context of dissimilar sociocultural experiences, and knowledge that school serves certain individuals and families better than others, the current stress on the educative role of the family, narrowly defined in terms of accountability in relation to school goals, represents a sharp and alarming shift. At this moment, it seems that the ideology of the social purposes of education is being adjusted, with an increased emphasis on social efficiency (Labaree, 1997), expressed by the *need* to train new work skills, produce improved outcomes, and raise test scores. Neo-liberal politics is attacking state bureaucracy and shrinking its social services, in favor of private, supposedly more efficient, small-scale, initiatives (Chubb & Moe, 1990). Within the rhetoric of new standards for education and production, and a better educated workforce for international economic competition, in order to maintain or boost the domestic quality of life as well as the leading political role of this nation in the world scenario, the blaming game of who is responsible for the present social crisis (poverty, unemployment, drug consuming, violence, alienation, customarily treated not as economic but as educational problems) seems to be shifting from the school to the family. More visible reforms like *school choice* and less visible ones like *more homework* have passed the burden onto the family, ignoring the concrete impact that the crisis has already had on the majority of families. The very fact that families are the most vulnerable to such crisis is taken for granted.

It seems that an attempt at establishing a novel educational mode is at work, with the redefinition of the very meaning of public education. The traditional model of public school, in which the family delegated education to the state but still retained autonomy in home education, is being pressed to be substituted by a model in which the state delegates education to the family or organized groups, while it still controls the standards, that is, determines the curriculum and administers the tests, just like Coleman's (1967) *open schools* model. Although the traditional model had been subverted by middle-class school control, it is important to reclaim its most important aspect: the commitment to equal treatment of students, including compensatory approaches (positive discrimination), and the goal to equalize basic outcomes.

In contrast, the model pressed to be generalized now seems to be that of the private school, which has survived, on a small scale, during the expansion of the public school system, or that of the privatized public school where families shop for a tailored education. Partnerships between school and family are only possible where there exists enough consensus over purposes, meanings, values, contents, and methods of instruction, and especially over the particular roles of teachers and parents—an experience that is more likely to occur in the context of private schools, where the school functions as an extension of the family, and/or where the exchange of money for service is quite direct and, by the way, where parents see teachers as subordinates.

The private school model also might accommodate cultural diversity better, insofar as it divides the greater community into small groups sharing common particular interests, while it eradicates the space of commonality represented by the unitarian public school, the only space available for the production and reproduction of democratic (communitarian) values and practices on a daily basis. Considering certain features of American society, like the recent history of school racial segregation, and the urban geography of class and ethnic segregation, this model might as well bring about resegregation on class, race, and ethnic lines.

It is redundant to say that the current policy redefinition of the meaning of the public school, the purpose of family education, and the role of parents in schooling, are not auspicious for many, underprivileged families. It is sensible to expect that any families under adverse circumstances, including middle-class families, will have their children's opportunities restricted, at the outset, by a policy and instructional practice requiring more parental involvement in school and specific academic forms of work at home. Yet, in recognizing the limits of families as educators, it is important to understand how relations between families and schools were initially constructed, and why families need schools, in spite of their defects.

Under the present conditions of social reproduction, though schooling has distinct meanings for different social groups, schools have a tangible meaning and an essential role, place, and time in the organization of daily life, beyond the use value of education outcomes and the exchange value of school credentials. The majority of families and parents, especially working class and poor minority, depend on the public school for the care, occupation, and education of children, and cannot substitute it (reversing history), or create a private alternative (like home schooling). Indeed, public education does not need to be compulsory anymore. As a central apparatus of social reproduction, schools became indispensable, for they keep children and youth while parents work, even if they fail to accomplish their claimed social purposes and specific academic, civic, and work training functions. This is, of course, a problematic issue in its own right, insofar as the expansion of its psychosocial function, in order to compensate for family weaknesses, has come in detriment of its academic function, which is precisely what most families, by definition, cannot provide.

Parenting as Symbolic Capital

In this era of extreme formalization of education and scientific regulation of human experience, certain trivial and informal kinds of knowledge and skills have been refurbished as special training, packed as courses and books, and sold under the rubric of continual and life-long education, expanding the educational market so to fit a variety of knowledges on how-to-do, how-to-succeed, and even how-to-enjoy things. This movement is not restricted to labor-market adjustments but has penetrated private life, fixing expectations and behaviors, blurring distinctions between leisure and study, subjecting personal expression and enrichment to assessment and normalization, thanks to the popularization of psychology and the great expansion of its professional market. Among such new *teachable* knowledges is *parenting*, which turned from an informal art of raising children (in a communitarian mode) into a science, with standardized and expert-prescribed contents and techniques (to be learned and applied in an individual mode).

Indeed, psychology has continually redefined positive and negative parenting and has considerably influenced family lifestyle, especially middle-class well-informed, *up-to-date* patterns of childrearing. A good indicator of the specialization and rationalization of parenting is the number of popular magazines featuring the issue, ranging from traditional to alternative approaches, and covering a variety of tastes and situations: *Child, Parenting, Family Life, Visitation* (the source for nontraditional families), *Mothering* (the magazine of natural family living), *Family Fun, Exceptional Parent* (the magazine for families and professionals), *Working Mother*, and *Parents* (Schuler Books, May, 1997).

Schools, in turn, have furthered and reinforced new demands for the education of children, and for the re-education of parents in the role of educating their own children, insofar as a certain parenting style is perceived as influential on school achievement. Thus, beyond providing for physical care, affective expression, and moral direction, parenting has assumed a very instrumental sense in that it is supposed to generate specific qualities and competencies fit to social opportunities and exchangeable for social rewards. It has been redefined as a specialized form of affective relationship explicitly required to be effective in the psychosocial development and, increasingly, in the cognitive development of children.

Parenting has both implicit and explicit dimensions that function as symbolic capital in current family–school exchanges. The implicit dimension is evident in the following typical family scene: The student comes home from school and the parent (usually mother) is eager to know how was the school day and what is the homework; next, the parent reads the homework, stimulates the student to do it and, if necessary, coaches him or her. In this way, cultural capital (in the form of a specific academic disposition) is developed. The explicit dimension, equivalent to social capital, is played in the school site by participation in various activities, which demonstrate that the parent is involved in his child's education and supportive of the school's agenda, and create the likelihood of profit in the form of a favorable disposition, on the part of teachers and principals, toward a particular student.

The centrality of the intellectual project within the definition and practice of middle-class parenting is explained by Bourdieu (1977) in the context of cultural and social reproduction: "Those sections which are richest in cultural capital are more inclined to invest in their children's education at the same time as in cultural practices liable to maintain and increase their specific rarity" (p. 502), thus integrating the investments placed in the academic career of their children into the system of strategies of its own (class) reproduction. Furthermore,

> ... the support accorded by a category to academic sanctions and hierarchies depends not only on the rank the school system grants to it in its hierarchies but also on the extent to which its interests are linked to the school system or, in other words, on the extent to which its commercial value and its social position depend (in the past as in the future) on academic approval ...
> (Bourdieu, 1977, p. 504)

Thus, consonant with current definitions of good parenting, middle-class parents have played quite a visible role in their children's education and consistently intervened in schooling as academic success is part of their lifestyle. Moreover, in their exchanges with the school they have relied not only on their own cultural capital, but on social capital as well: the "right presentation" and "the manners and taste resulting from good breeding, which, in certain careers . . . , constitute the condition, if not the principal factor, of success" (Bourdieu, 1977, p. 506).

Lareau's (1993) empirical findings depicted the efforts of upper middle-class, professional families in constructing their children's school success. She argued that "social class (independent of ability) does affect schooling. Teachers ask for parent involvement, social class shapes the resources which parents have at their disposal to comply with teachers' requests for assistance" (p. 2). Hence, teaching (the form of pedagogic work carried by the school) is articulated with a particular (productive) parenting model. The way schools are conceived and organized, teachers not only *need* parental commitment to academic activities and encourage parents' engagement with homework, but they also make decisions concerning students based on evaluations—or rather bets, involving stereotypes and prejudices—about their parents.

On the side of the family, social class provides differentiated resources that are needed to fit the current model of schooling—the family–school partnership, in which the family is supposed to fulfill an auxiliary, but rather basic, academic function. Those resources, basically economic, as already noted, are concentrated on the time, and cultural and social capital of the mother. In fact, as acknowledged by David (1980, 1989), home–school relations are broadly and specifically built into gender-differentiated parenting roles. In the absence of collective or state responsibility, mothers are usually the sole responsible parent for children during preschool years (prior to the age of compulsory schooling), before and after school hours daily, and during school breaks and vacations, which do not coincide with the length of the working day and working year.

Lareau (1993) also verified empirically that, although gender neutral, parenting really means mostly *mothering*: "parent involvement remains primarily mother involvement in education while fathers, particularly in upper middle class homes, have an important symbolic role" (p. 95); while "contemporary mothers appear to face a more varied, complex, and labor-intensive set of tasks in promoting their children's academic progress than in previous eras," fathers exert a leadership role in important educational decisions and inter-institutional pursuits, such as formal complaints to school (pp. 90–95). In effect, this "pattern of maternal activity and paternal passivity" (p. 88) reflects differentiated gender roles within the family, where women play reproductive roles complementary to men's central role as economic providers, which is especially true for the upper middle-class, where mothering may constitute women's sole or principal career. Therefore, the model of parenting envisioned by parental involvement policies, characterized by a strong intellectual accent, is typical of the schooled middle class, which counts on mothers' intensive and extensive dedication to overseeing their children's schooling, and bringing home activities in alignment with the school curriculum (Fine, 1993; Lareau, 1993). As invisible and devalued female work, mothering is just not acknowledged as the core of parental involvement.

On the side of the school, it seems correct to state that *social class (and parental ability) affects schooling the more teachers ask for parent involvement in preparing for, complementing, and reinforcing instruction.* Insofar as teachers' success depends on effective parenting, it also seems reasonable to state that teachers will depend all the more on parental commitment to school success the more they are pressured to raise outcomes and the less they actually dispose of time and efficient pedagogic resources to promote learning independent of parental support. It is fair to assume that—as a rule, special compensatory programs being the exception—schools and teachers are organized to count on parental academic support, as the current formalization of parental involvement into a policy attests. Consequently, a policy attempting to mobilize parental academic support is doomed to consecrate family education alignment to school standards (what makes no difference to and actually benefits certain groups), as well as recognize certain parents' efforts to increment their own children's school experience (what has typically happened within the middle and upper classes).

Eventually, the mystique of good parenting may be used as an asset in the struggle for school success also by lower class parents, as suggested by Lareau's (1993) rich data. The following events, which occurred in a working-class school with low levels and few kinds of parental involvement (as compared to an upper middle-class school), illustrate the cling between parents' performance and institutional discrimination imbedded in the structure and culture of the school and actualized in teachers' practices, particularly in their expectations and judgments about effective parenting and potential student success.

A first grade (female) teacher was impressed by the parents—particularly the father—of a (male) student and concluded (also based on other performance data) that "Johnny's parents had worked with him at home, reading to him, teaching him new words, and giving him educational *advantages*" (Lareau, 1993, p. 141). Then, "despite her conviction that Johnny was not a gifted student and her knowledge that he was only slightly above the class average, Mrs. Thompson recommended that he be selected for the school enrichment program." However, she "did not recommend that children with similar, or even slightly superior, academic records be admitted to the program" (p. 142). Lareau (1993) suggested that "Johnny's parents may have influenced her decision . . . [and that] his parents' behavior raised her expectations" (p. 142).

A second grade (female) teacher "believed strongly that children's home environments influenced their classroom performance" (Lareau, 1993, p. 142). She heard rumors about a (female) student's mother who had frequent parties at home and *neglected* her child, and concluded that "because of her home situation, Anne-Marie did not have as positive an attitude toward school as children whose parents were more conventional" (p. 142). Despite the fact that this student had a top performance and "greater reading fluency when reading aloud than most of her peers, Mrs. Sampson did not focus on her reading skills until the end of the year, when she looked at the standardized test scores" (p. 143). According to Lareau's (1993) analysis,

> . . . it is possible, even likely, that Mrs. Sampson's negative assessment of Anne-Marie's home life clouded her view of the child's classroom performance . . . until challenged by test scores. With other children . . . [especially a Vietnamese boy and a sheriff's daughter] Mrs. Sampson appeared to expect good performance and was on the lookout for evidence of academic promise. (p. 143)

Thus, whereas in the lower class school Lareau (1993) discovered that "children's schooling—particularly their access to special programs—could be shaped more by teachers' perceptions of the parents' role in education than by the children's performance in the classroom," at the upper middle-class school she found "no signs . . . of teachers—on their own initiative—altering a child's school program based on their assessment of the students' parents' values" (p. 143).

The counterpart of parental involvement is teacher positive discrimination— noninvolvement resulting in negative discrimination. As Lareau (1993) states, while parents' actions "appeared to influence teachers' assessment of children's abilities and their potential for achievement" (p. 141), in turn "when teachers believed that parents valued education and were heavily involved in children's schooling, they took actions which they did not take for children whose parents were less active in schooling" (p. 140). This is understandable in terms that the logic of the school and its agents is also a logic of investment and profit, minimization of time and effort (and frustration), and maximization of success and gains. Hence, automatic and unconscious reading by the teacher of signs of cultural, social, and economic capital, orient decisions regarding the capitalization on the apparent *habitus* of the student.

Moreover, Lareau (1993) observed that "the tone, breadth, and quality" (p. 105) of teacher–parent interactions differed between the working-class and upper middle-class schools: more stilted in the former and more relaxed in the latter, a feature not attributable to teachers' treatment. She also noted that the working class school had three formal programs of parental involvement (a read-at-home program, a parent education workshop, and a class on parenting for single parents), and that the teachers there "were more vigorous . . . in recruiting parents to work with their children at home" (p. 106). In contrast, the upper middle-class school had a very active parents' club, which sponsored fund-raising activities and a classroom volunteer program (giving parents opportunities to learn about instructional activities, their children's performance within the group, and teachers' performance, as well).

Quite surprisingly, Lareau (1993) denied the occurrence of institutional discrimination, for teachers did not "make different requests of parents or, even in subtle ways, encourage upper middle-class parents to be involved more than working-class parents" (p. 104). The way she posed the issue is already revealing of a particular arbitrary stance: Parental involvement is positive, hence all parents should be equally encouraged to get involved, which leaves the choice, merit or fault, to them. By limiting potential discrimination to a discrete moment (teachers' first move), she missed its dynamic (as if all was left to parents' initiative), as well as the prior point that the conditions for (further) discrimination are already embedded in the very request of parental involvement.

Policy Prospects

As education involves the workings of family and school, amid a multitude of other powerful social influences, such as mass media communications, educational policy can be conceived precisely as a framework connecting their interactions in favor of public goals. However, in regard to school–family relations, it is important to recognize that educational policy has fundamentally carried the politics of schooling that, nonetheless, has served differently the politics of education of diverse families. In the past, whereas school policy did not deal directly and explicitly with family education, parent–teacher–principal interactions were left to random individual initiatives within traditional local politics, what worked well for certain groups and individuals. What is new now, and needs to be acknowledged, is that state policy is not only expanding its scope of action by formalizing those interactions and by specifying the educational contribution of the family toward schooling, but is also regulating family–school relations according to one particular model: the middle-class pattern of parental involvement.

    This new movement articulates family policy with school policy, seemingly on behalf of all children and under a framework of social efficiency, in complicated and contradictory ways. Although it is generally expected that public policy should deal with the school and not interfere with the private realm of family education, a policy like parental involvement in schooling tends to raise immediate agreement and even enthusiasm. It sounds correct because it draws on parents' natural obligation; it sounds good because it aims at benefiting children; and it sounds desirable because it will increase democratic participation and raise school achievement. Moreover, it echoes the middle-class cultural tradition, specifically the belief that families, that is, parents, influence school policy. Nevertheless, besides specific conditions and dispositions of parents to participate, such a policy presupposes what it aims at building: cultural continuity and identity of purposes between all families and schools—a doubtful prerequisite in times of acute cultural diversity and conflict (Berliner, 1997; Hunter, 1991).

    A basic contradictory aspect refers to the family–school division of educational work. If it is consensual that both families and schools educate, the intersections and boundaries of their roles have not been stable or thoroughly clear. On the one hand, setting aside the fact that schooling builds on a particular family–class culture (Bourdieu & Passeron, 1977), according to the traditional delegation model, teachers should not expect more from parents than physical and emotional care, so that children can come to school prepared to learn its curriculum. Apparently, the *crisis of the family* (stressed parents, working mothers, divorces, burdened single parents, lack of quantity and quality time with children) has reduced its role in physical, emotional, social, and moral discipline, requiring schools, in turn, to extend their traditional role in academic and civic instruction in order to encompass various bio-psychosocial aspects. In this context, it is inconceivable to attribute the family a role in academic education. On the other hand, setting aside the latent conflict between parents and teachers (Waller, 1965), it seems reasonable to count on parents and to expect them to be teachers' best allies in schooling, as parents desire the best for their children and would be willing to help teachers' efforts in various ways. But this supposes a few conditions: that the parents dispose of time, interest, and know-how in order to help; that they are familiar with the school culture and value the school curriculum; and that they submit to teachers' authority and lead. Granted these conditions, parents' work for schooling, with moral and emotional obligation as an incentive, would have the advantage of bearing no direct costs for the school. And, in case parents needed to be taught how to help, it would have perhaps the additional advantage of creating special projects, new grants, and specialized jobs in the school and academy.

A related contradictory aspect pertains to teacher authority. In the delegation model, family authority and school authority are separate, teacher authority being enacted over the student in the limits of the classroom, without parental mediation. In the partnership model, on the contrary, teachers may exert authority over the parents, as the latter mediate between schoolwork and homework, but resent parental interference in their professional camp. Another cost for teachers may derive from the new obligation to consult, coordinate, and evaluate parents' homework. Moreover, a teacher–parent partnership may invite two peculiar situations: one in which teacher and parent dispute instructional choices, or compete for influence over the child, and another in which they become accomplices in pressuring the child. Of course there can be happy cases in which teacher, parent, and child get along well, but there can be also unlucky relationships having to last for a whole school year! So, although sometimes students might benefit from a teacher–parent alliance, they can also benefit from the difference between the adults' approaches. The contradiction for teachers is that they need and like parents' interest, support, and appreciation, but they are better off with the delegation model.

Why do teachers need parental involvement? I firmly believe that when teachers have good work conditions, and students learn satisfactorily, they do not need to engage ordinarily with parents. Teachers have needed parental backing when they feel impotent and frustrated. And they have typically blamed the family for student failure because they are also subject to blame from principals and parents, and moreover because they lack the practical and intellectual means to develop an effective social, institutional, and pedagogic critique, due to the very function and conditions of their work. For the essential contradiction of teachers' work is that they are supposed to help students learn and, at the same time, to assess them negatively and fail them, in the name of meritocracy, or with the purpose of helping them further. Parents, in turn, do not need to get involved in schooling as long as all is going well, and they normally prefer to trust teachers and leave the job to them. There are also gains in maintaining a distance from school and its demands, as parent–child relations can be more relaxing and enjoyable if they do not spin around school subjects, homework, quizzes, and grades.

Another potential source of tensions may derive from parental conceptions of education and perceptions of schooling. From the perspective of the family, parental involvement in education and in schooling are, indeed, two different things that might fit or crash. As long as there is agreement over the content and quality of education offered by schools (i.e., parental tacit support) and satisfactory student outcomes (i.e., convergence of individual achievement and institutional efficiency), all is well, but if learning is perceived as deficient, either in individual or institutional terms, or if it conflicts with family values, then there is a situation of crisis. Albeit the continual rhetoric of school crisis might be, to a great extent, fabricated, as Berliner and Biddle (1995) argued, there is disagreement over the content of schooling in U.S. society, and discontent over its quantitative and/or qualitative outcomes among various groups, either conservative or progressive. In such cases, participation in school may ensue from parents' initiative, either individually in attempting to get a tailored education for a particular child, or collectively organized around a specific change agenda, as for instance the current movement against outcome-based education (Luksik & Hoffecker, 1995). Parents may also try to compensate for schools' lacks by private means even radically withdrawing from public education as exemplified by the home schooling movement.

Therefore, the main contradiction of parental involvement in schooling as a policy is that, albeit wrapped as grassroots, it is really top–down. But, of course, this is not likely to be perceived by those who are on top or share in its logic (the cultural arbitrary where it is nested). As parental involvement basically depends on consensus over purposes and contents of schooling, and on coincidence between parents' educational conceptions and possibilities, and school goals and practices, ultimately this policy bears upon the hierarchical relation between school knowledge and family diverse cultures with the equity implications already suggested.

Alternatively, what would a policy concerned with equity pose in terms of school purposes and family–school relations? In order to answer this question it is important to retrieve two fundamental points: the democratic ideal of education and the social function of schooling.

Recalling Bourdieu and Passeron's (1977) theoretical contribution, the educational system fulfills relatively stable social functions: It plays a key role in cultural and social reproduction by inflating or deflating students' initial cultural capital acquired from family and class socialization, and converting it (or not) into more or less valued credentials. The individual path to profitable exchanges and school success depends on *familiarity* with the school's specific knowledge, language, and standards of evaluation, and reflects the distance or affinity between home and class culture (informal education) and academic culture (the formal school curriculum). Thus, the production of educational failure is intrinsic to the functioning of an educational system that encompasses individuals from diverse cultural backgrounds, but implicitly adopts one cultural framework. Consequently, policies that leave these particular reproductive mechanisms untouched necessarily promote educational and social inequality by reinforcing the existing structure of the distribution of cultural capital among the social classes.

Moreover, a policy that misrecognizes the fact that both material and cultural resources are pre-conditions for successful alignment to the educational mode of the dominant culture, that is, omits the fact that a certain initial cultural capital (produced, transmitted, and inherited within particular social conditions) is required to invest in and benefit from the school mode, and explicitly demands family alignment to the school, is assigning the family not only entire responsibility for student success, but also a role (an improper political role) in minimizing educational and social inequalities, inequalities which the family does not produce or reproduce per se. Thus, it seems obvious that a policy that prescribes the educative role of families in relation to school goals is likely to create more inequity, as schools (which have properly a political role) organize their pedagogical processes counting on the implicit and explicit support of families.

Social equality and individual self-realization are ideals and aspirations. The fact that they have not come true does not diminish their power in orienting human pursuits and inspiring the educational agenda. The limited powers of both families and schools in promoting them have to be acknowledged so that alternatives can be devised.

Once the political–structural limits of schooling, in particular, are acknowledged, the issue of realizing its specific symbolic power remains. Reproduction does allow for a range of choices (and ideological disputes) in terms of knowledge and practices. Bourdieu and Passeron's (1977) framework showed that, as the school constitutes a symbolic market in itself (in that it mediates between preceding individual and family inequality and broader, parallel, and subsequent economic and symbolic structures), it has some degree of autonomy to influence the processes and outcomes of its own production—the space of production in reproduction. And, indeed, symbolic violence may be practiced in various degrees and forms. As it constitutes a setting of symbolic exchanges and conflicts, the school has also, *ideally*, to conciliate between the dissemination of a common culture (the dominant cultural arbitrary, in any case) and respect for diverse individuals and cultures, through (as much as possible) democratic processes, such as socio-interactionist instructional methods. Consequently, educational policies and practices represent a range of choices in reducing or augmenting the dependence of students' opportunities upon their social origins, in breaking or fastening the *automatic* conversion of family and class material and cultural differences into school success or failure. The fecundity of pedagogy resides precisely in thinking over the possibilities of *conversion of symbolic capital*, in the terrain of cultural diversity.

Along this line, an alternative policy framework for family–school relations, aiming at producing a more equalizing effect, should initially frame the relations between these distinct institutions as nonessential and accessory, that is, entirely optional, recognizing family educational practices as diverse and autonomous, while clearly demarcating the specificity of the pedagogic work (purposes and knowledge) of the school. Because the crucial issue of family–school interactions is cultural, referring to the reproduction of a cultural arbitrary and implying the demarcation of the knowledge to be imposed upon all and assessed in the context of schooling, the problem can be defined, from the perspective of the family, as to what extent school offers valuable knowledge and succeeds in imparting it, while simultaneously allowing for the co-existence of diverse cultures and knowledges in the family and community realms.

In contrast, the education encompassed by schooling is distinctively political and fundamentally distinct from—and not necessarily continuous with—the education provided by diverse families. Therefore, a project of educational equity must initially recognize and respect families' differentiated resources and choices, and clearly delimit the school's educative mission in terms of imparting a common and special knowledge within its own time, space and resources, while compensating for family knowledge differentials and assessing only what it explicitly and systematically offers. In other words, instead of counting on the educational workings of the family, the school should work ways to precisely discount family educational input from its educational output by investing in effective pedagogic processes, consequently liberating families from any form of educational accountability defined by school policy and practice.

It is useful to recall here Bourdieu and Passeron's (1977) point that the efficiency of modes of inculcation, that is, an effective pedagogy, "cannot be defined independently from the content inculcated and the social functions which the pedagogic work in question fulfills in a determinate social formation" (p. 47). School social selection is exercised based on both imposition of an exclusive (unfamiliar, irrelevant) knowledge and negation of access to its code to the majority of students. In this light, as pointed out by Gagnon (1995), the role of a core curriculum and universal standards is crucial for equality: Only by defining "the basics" of public education, as a clear intellectual project, can its proper pedagogic role be strengthened. Thus, insofar as the *differential productivity of schooling, according to ethnic group and social class, is produced by the very exercise of its pedagogic work*, which excludes those who lack the capital and ethos objectively presupposed by its mode of inculcation, the school then must *produce as much as possible the conditions for its own productivity*, that is, *invest in effective teaching–learning methods, without relying in preconditions produced elsewhere*.

Finally, without a critical view of the function of the educational system in reproducing social inequality through its implicit partnership with one model of family, and through the very exercise of its specific forms of pedagogic work, it is not possible to see the false promise of parental involvement as a policy and generalizable practice. For one thing, the strategy of reaching the family in order to capitalize on family (differentiated) resources as a way to simultaneously reduce state investments in education, enhance student achievement and school productivity, and better educate all children seems rather tortuous. The practical forms and effects of this mandated partnership may be to create more complications for both schools and families, and to amplify educational inequity, in spite of good intentions. Therefore, since it is quite doubtful that educational policy can exert a more equalizing effect by focusing on the family, it should definitely avoid intervention in the family realm and refocus on the learning environment and purposes of the school.

4

The Obscure Side of Homework

From the school perspective, homework may be considered an educational need, a segment of instruction and of the school curriculum, and a policy. It has long been known as an instructional strategy. Traditionally, it has been used as drill and review (application and evaluation exercises), and as preparation (mostly through readings) for classes and exams. Its content has mostly derived from the school curriculum, and occasionally has included creative exercises, like journal writing focusing on students' personal experiences, and special projects, under the rubric of curriculum enrichment. It has also been conceived as a strategy of linking school contents and *real* (social) life, eventually focusing on family and community activities and events, or even television programs. On the psychosocial and moral aspects, homework has been justified in terms of building independence and responsibility through the development of study habits and punctuality. Finally, as a policy measure, it has been considered a panacea for raising student achievement and generally improving the quality of schooling.

Once acknowledged as a need and a legitimate strategy of instruction and educational policy, homework appears as a topic in need of continual elaboration and assessment, employing teachers, researchers, and policymakers. Thus, textbooks must contain homework sections; instructional packs must provide home problem-solving suggestions; content, form, and purpose of homework must undergo revision and assessment; and explicit homework policies must be enforced. Homework also appears as a problem of motivation and compliance: some students resist or procrastinate, some parents omit or neglect. It arises as a problem that cannot be easily solved by means of school resources.

As an integral part of instruction, homework not only affects its planning and implementation, but it also affects the lives of students outside school and their family routines, as it supposes a time–space–knowledge conceptual frame connecting classroom and home activities. Thus, defined as the principal means of home–school connections, conceived either as a learning problem or solution, homework is inseparable from family–school relationships in the context of their

115

common and specific social and educational purposes and responsibilities. These relationships have been recently addressed by the policy of *parental involvement* that corroborates homework as parental obligation (National Education Goals Panel, 1995). However, it is fundamental to question the notion of homework as an educational need, and its broad pedagogical and social implications.

While homework has become a formal policy, there has been an informal politics of homework played by students' families. Indeed, from the family point of view, homework may be seen either as a legitimate need and a desirable practice, or as a burden and an imposition, depending on variable material and symbolic conditions of diverse families. Yet, family conditions and aspirations may be expressed overtly as politics-practices in favor of homework by parents as actors, in accordance with school politics-practices (i.e., concrete demands for parental support), whereas contrary feelings are more likely to remain covert.

There are various interesting aspects of the policy-practice of homework related to instructional conceptions and forms, and the work of teachers. There are also less visible but very important aspects related to the evolution of the educational practices of families and schools, the redefinition of boundaries and functions (or overlay and tangle) of private and public realms of social life as educative contexts, and the *homework* of parents or, more precisely, mothers. On the one hand, the predominant conception and practice of homework as schoolwork transferred to the home might constitute a defensive strategy of school accountability, insofar as schools might not be doing their specific job, that is, providing children (enough) formal education. On the other hand, it might offer a pertinent illustration of symbolic violence (Bourdieu & Passeron, 1977) via the extension of the pedagogic authority of the school (entrusted with the function of imposition of the dominant cultural arbitrary) to the home—in other words, a case of public policy regulating private life via the instruction or discipline of the family by the school, through the imposition of the canonical curriculum and both explicit and implicit prescription of parenting practices. This is most visible when homework becomes a strategy of mainstreaming minority, immigrant, and/or working-class families.

In order to develop my argument, I offer a brief historical, research and policy overview, followed by a discussion of conceptions and implications of homework for learning and assessment, teacher work, family life, and school achievement. Finally, I stress the role of homework in connecting school and family in various—often conflicting and contradictory—ways, and propose that instruction be conceived independently from family input under the form of homework. Acknowledging the differences between home- and school-specific contexts, knowledges, and practices, as well as conceiving the possibility of distance between school and family in a positive (i.e., clear and productive) way, may provide more focus on classroom processes and school resources, as well as on pedagogical alternatives in developing the academic curriculum for the benefit of all students (and especially of those considered disadvantaged). At the same time, it may allow for the conservation of diverse family and social group cultures, and may be both more just and less harmful for children and parents, and also for teachers, in the end.

ORIGINS AND RECENT DEVELOPMENTS OF THE HOMEWORK ISSUE

When child learning occurred in the realms of family, community, and economic production, before the advent of the common compulsory school, *homework* was practical and productive work done at home. Later, when school attendance became normal, schools that served rural communities and early urban industrial settings did not customarily send work home, because it would take students away from *real* work and, thus, affect their families' survival needs.

Throughout the 20th century, the very use of the term *homework as schoolwork sent home* suggested that academic learning had not remained confined to school, and appeared as the most appropriate occupation of youngsters. However, home learning aligned to the school curriculum is not a general or natural family practice, but part of the lifestyle of the schooled social classes. This assumes a problematic character in the face of the ideal of democratic education, according to which the school constitutes the social space where all students, provided equal opportunities, share a common educational experience and are evaluated in terms of a specific (common) curriculum, despite diverse family and social class background cultures. From this point of view, homework will variably affect school performance, because home conditions are not controlled by the school.

In effect, there has been dispute about the importance of homework in U.S. education throughout this century (Gill & Schlossman, 1995). Homework has been recurrently advanced or retracted as a matter of educational discourse and policy, not only as a result of debates over pedagogical conceptions, but also as a result of family pressures (M. Sedlak, personal communication, April 1995). Its amount and forms, for instance, have been regulated by school policy—probably, as a consequence of parents' informal politics—as homework has been variously devised as a strategy to raise academic standards or perceived as interfering with family life and individual students' social activities.

The Progressives, who emphasized interest and joy versus will and effort (R. Prawatt, personal communication, April 1995), did not support homework policies associated with *traditional* learning methods. According to Gill and Schlossman (1995, p. B7), "in the decades before World War II, many school districts (including Los Angeles) abolished homework, ostensibly in order to discourage rote learning in the classroom and encourage more creative use of non-school hours by children and families." At that time, as a clear expression of middle-class values, research attempted to prove that homework did not help school achievement and, moreover, that it harmed children:

> Reformers denounced homework, first of all, as a threat to children's health. The Ladies' Home Journal carried on a lengthy crusade, offering its readers sordid tales from parents, teachers and doctors about the alleged harms (including death) caused by overworking children. (Gill & Schlossman, 1995, p. B7)

In the 1950s, however, pro-homework positions succeeded in the educational debate and policy amid general dissatisfaction and attacks on progressive education, a renewed stress on academic rigor and excellence, and the urge to surpass the Soviet Union in the context of the cold war. The conservative stress on excellence had also been appealing to the middle classes insofar as a higher quality education conferred distinction to its bearers. There is evidence that homework then had already turned into formal school policy (Lankton & Rasscharet, 1961). Epps (1966), for instance, acknowledged an increasing tendency to view homework as an integral part of schoolwork.

During the civil rights movement of the 1960s, the belief in the relevance of homework was boosted by studies comparing high and low achievers from different socioeconomic and ethnic backgrounds. Low achievers were found to be inner-city kids, from poor, single-parent homes, members of ethnic minorities such as Blacks and Mexican Americans, and obviously economically disadvantaged and *culturally unprepared* to take advantage of social resources. High achievers originated from white middle- and upper-class stable families, and eventually from certain ethnic groups as Asian Americans, who had incorporated formal education as part of their lifestyle or as a means of social mobility. Thus, low achievers and their families became the target of compensatory education policy aimed at improving their home learning environments and family culture by combining homework and parent education, under the banner of equity (Scott-Jones, 1984, 1987, 1993). Yet, according to Gill and Schlossman (1995), the anti-homework tradition appeared again to shape policy and practice during the 1970s: "By the mid-1970s, American high schools assigned far less homework than they had fifteen years earlier; hardly anyone complained" (p. B7).

In the 1980s, with the publication of *A Nation at Risk* by the National Commission on Excellence in Education (1983), which credited the U.S. political, economical and moral downfall to a *soft pedagogy* (Gill & Schlossman, 1995), pro-homework views gained prominence once more. International comparative studies also reinforced the perception of the importance of family environment and homework practices, as Japanese, Chinese, and Taiwanese students were found to perform better in standardized tests and do more hours of homework per week than U.S. students (Stevenson & Stigler, 1992). Although research, overall, was scarce and inconclusive (Epstein & Pinkow, 1988), common sense derived from homework tradition (nested in the ideology of family values and hard work) converged with the stress on homework as a strategy to increase school productivity in face of the urgency to surpass economic competitors, according to the national (international hegemony) political framework. There is evidence to suggest that the 1980s saw an expansion of formal homework policies throughout the country's school districts and buildings (ERIC Abstracts Data Base; Connecticut State Department of Education, 1984; Conover, 1990; Doyle & Barber, 1990; Foyle & Lyman, 1989; Los Angeles Unified School District, 1983; Murphy & Decker, 1989; San Mateo County Office of Education, 1983), as homework for all students was highlighted amidst a series of reforms aiming at academic excellence, especially during the first part of the decade (Chubb & Moe, 1990; Roderique et al., 1994).

Accordingly, the educational rhetoric of the 1990s, following (or resisting) the education productivity-privatization trend, has strongly emphasized family accountability and school choice—alternatively, parental empowerment and increased participation in school reform. On the one hand, policy advertises a correlation between student achievement (especially in mathematics and science), individual competitiveness (better jobs), and international competitiveness (U.S. political-economic leadership in the world; Arbanas, 1994; Ingham Intermediate School District, 1995). On the other hand, national official guidelines prescribe regular homework as a strategy to improve academic performance (Office of Educational Research and Improvement, 1992, 1996), extending educational policy to the home, as suggestions of limiting TV viewing, enhancing reading, and monitoring homework clearly transfer learning accountability to the parental sphere. In spite of the policy call for broad school–family partnerships (Goal 8, cited in National Education Goals Panel, 1995), parental participation on a daily and continual basis appears mostly restricted to the homework issue.

As for research, although it has reproduced, in part, the historical controversy over the value of homework, there seems to be clear preponderance of favorable evaluations of the impact of homework on achievement (ERIC Abstracts Data Base). While learning disabilities and compensatory education programs are significantly visible areas of investigation on parental involvement and homework, a considerable amount of research, fostered by a demand for *homework productivity*, has focused on motivational and valuational aspects related to students and families, and on task conceptual relevance related to instructional planning and assessment.

In effect, the positive impact of homework on academic achievement (as a single variable correlated with increased test scores) has not been (and, indeed, can hardly be) empirically or experimentally established, but few studies make this explicit while providing pro-homework policy recommendations (e.g., Palardy, 1988). One research, for instance, has pointed out the smaller direct effect of homework on achievement, as compared to powerful direct effects of intellectual ability and academic coursework, in the case of high school students (Keith & Cool, 1992), but most studies (based on specific local intervention) continue to assume a general positive correlation between homework and achievement whatever the grade level. Overall, there is not substantial or sufficient research to support correlations between high achievement, time spent on homework, kinds of assignment, and tutoring styles, across grades, curricular goals, subjects, levels of student ability, and individual, socioeconomic and ethnic group characteristics. Nevertheless, research continues to generate favorable policy prescriptions, whereas studies that focus on the limits, difficulties or disadvantages of homework are incipient (e.g., Cooper, 1994; Hossler, Stage, & Gallagher, 1988; Palardy, 1988, 1995). This is a case in which cultural (implicit) assumptions direct research problem and conceptual choices (and, consequently, results), legitimating policy-political trends through scientific apparatus.

Accordingly, policy has focused both on homework conception and on parental implementation. A national survey of homework policies at school district level by Roderique et al. (1994) revealed that, although only 35.2% of U.S. school districts (N=267, 48.5% response) had a policy on homework at that moment, 91.1% informed parents about homework policies and regulations; 51.1% specified the types of assignment (class preparation, practice exercises, completion of tasks and extension activities); 48.8% provided guidelines for teacher feedback (letter grades, constructive comments and praise, numeric grades, and added incentives); 58.2% specified roles that parents are expected to assume in the homework process (provide space and time, monitor task completion, and sign completed work); and 35.2% had a specific policy including frequency (three to four nights a week), amount of daily assignments (41.5 minutes at elementary, 1 hour 7.8 minutes at middle, and 1 hour 40.2 minutes at high school levels), and home–school communication mechanisms.

Apparently, controversy over the appropriateness and fairness of homework has vanished at policy level, as schools are delivering explicit and comprehensive homework policies defining its rationale, school expectations, and parents' obligations. At a practical and close level, some schools reinforce the homework policy with the aid of *homework hotlines* (after school assistance through telephone), whereas many teachers start the year with a *contract* specifying homework obligations, to be signed by both student and parent, or adopt a *parent homework record*.

An example of up-to-date homework school policy follows:

Definition:
Homework refers to an assignment to be completed *outside of school hours preferably at home* [italics added]. These assignments keep parents informed and involved in their child's learning.
Policy:
Well chosen, clearly communicated homework is an *integral part of the instructional process* [italics added]. Challenging and relevant homework will be provided.
Homework assignments will *review, reinforce or extend classroom learning* [italics added] by providing practice and application of knowledge gained; *teach students responsibility* [italics added] and organizational skills; promote wise and orderly *use of time*; and *provide opportunities for enrichment activities* [italics added].
. . . School teachers will include homework appropriate for the students and their educational needs. Teachers will consider assignments of other teachers, *individual differences in students* [italics added], and other factors that may affect *the home as an extension of the classroom* [italics added].
Consequences for not completing homework will be handled by individual teachers [italics added]. Teachers may *detain a student(s) to complete homework after school* [italics added] on Monday, Wednesday or Thursday unless notified by the parent/guardian that the student(s) is not to be detained on any of those specific days. Also, if after-school homework completion is a consequence, for example, the students will know about it in advance

and, therefore, they will be held responsible for informing their parents about their after-school work. The late bus will be available for these students on Mondays, Wednesdays, and Thursdays. (East Lansing Educational Foundation, 1996, p. 14)

An interesting consequence of this type of policy is to hold parents formally accountable for noncompletion of homework, creating the likelihood of judicial battles between families and schools. Recently, *The Detroit News* (Murphy, 1996) featured the following headline: "School district to make detention a family affair." The district policy in question required parents to attend Saturday morning detention and do homework with their insubordinate kids, hence holding parents accountable for classroom misconduct. Legal measures to hold parents accountable, and "help them identify unwanted behavior patterns in their kids before they become bigger problems," were also anticipated, ranging from attending lectures on "how to better raise their children," to juvenile court hearings for students, and the arrest of the parents—conviction meaning 90 days in jail and a $500 fine—in case detention was refused and truancy thus established (Murphy, 1996, on-line). Such policies, unfortunately, are targeted at disadvantaged populations, making schooling a case of social discipline and punishment.

Finally, it is important to note the smaller amount of literature on alternative policy efforts and programs aimed at substituting for parental tutoring of homework. School initiatives have taken the form of after-school programs (e.g., Popwell, 1991), featuring "homework on-site supervision," a daily guided *in-school homework* practice (Locke, 1991), which curiously keeps the designation. Community support of homework includes public library homework centers, and other forms of *community homework centers* for at-risk students, which are suggestive of the limits of many families, especially working parents, in providing for the homework obligation.

INSTRUCTIONAL AND SOCIAL RELEVANCE

As an instructional strategy, homework is meant to extend learning, connect precedent and subsequent class work, stimulate independent study habits, and enrich the curriculum. It represents an important resource, which can potentially benefit all students. Yet, it is noteworthy that, although it is supposed to take place in the home, requiring that families reshape their activities around it, its content and form are designed at school, taking for granted the home conditions necessary for it to perform its function, that is, the function of helping all students learn the school curriculum in order to succeed.

The widespread belief in the relevance of homework for academic achievement is expressed through particular conceptions and practices related to distinct curricular goals. The predominant conception is that homework increases instructional time and the amount of curricular contents that the teacher can cover, so that student effort would build quality learning. Low-ability students, in particular, need more hours of work to catch up with expected standards. The quality and design of tasks could also enhance specific skills. An alternative conception seeks to connect school and home in order to broaden learning experiences, by attempting to integrate diverse aspects of family and community cultures to the school curriculum, and to connect and apply academic contents to everyday life.

Why is homework necessary? One plausible reason is the simple and obvious acknowledgement that school time is not enough to accomplish curricular goals (e.g., Doyle & Barber, 1990). Another answer, which confirms the previous, is that time spent on homework increases total learning time (of the school curriculum). However, the general institutionalization and acceptance of homework also suggests that schoolwork is viewed as a desirable occupation for children in the home (frequently in opposition to TV watching), and/or as a means of enabling children to raise their performance and compete in school and in future life. Along this line, it seems reasonable to consider that the school curriculum is positively valued, at least by those families and students who adhere to homework practices.

The meaning and value of homework are related to conceptions of education, valid and useful social knowledge, purposes of schools, and roles of families. Compulsory schooling involves an implicit *social contract* between families and the state, that is, a division of labor in the common task of educating children. The traditional division of educational work between school and family has posited intellectual development and the teaching of subject matter as the main function of schooling, while socialization and the formation of dispositions and values have constituted prerequisites basically developed in the home. Nevertheless, schools have needed to increasingly perform pychosocial roles, substituting for prior family functions and assuming a parental role (Elkind, 1995), which indicates that for many families the conditions of the traditional partnership were not viable.

Students' failure in completing homework and parents' unresponsiveness to school expectations may express that, for some students and parents, the terms of the contract may be unattainable and unfair. In such cases, the evident reasons are economic and cultural: parents' (and high school students') workloads and conflicting schedules, and values related to education and school originated from working class life experience. As educational needs and values conflict with survival needs and other values, families are unable to participate in this partnership. Yet, interestingly, policy efforts have focused on cultural approaches, such as involving (re-educating) parents, and practical approaches, such as providing extended day and Saturday enrichment programs, when not focusing on blatant punishment (often, detention; e.g., Conover, 1990), while maintaining homework. The whole instructional conception that includes homework has not yet been subject to radical questioning from a more inclusive outlook, one able to account for disadvantaged families and students' own perspectives.

Problems of low achievement and homework resistance do not affect all students. Nevertheless, homework is a *general policy*, based on the assumption that all children will profit from more schoolwork done at home. Apparently, the targets of the homework compensatory policy would be low achievers, but those students precisely lack the motivation, parental support, and other resources necessary to commit and benefit from it in the first place. The general prescription of homework, then, needs to be considered at the core of a certain curricular conception, which in turn needs to be considered within a broader framework of educational and social values and practices, which make up what Lareau (1993) called home advantage—that is, social class cultural capital.

The Articulation of Homework and Classwork

Within a strictly technical framework, conceiving instruction with or without homework affects classwork—and, of course, different conceptions of homework affect it differently. This is because the teacher has to figure ways to integrate homework and classwork, give specific homework feedback, and establish the relation of homework to evaluation and assessment within the learning process.

Within the traditional teaching–learning process, homework fits into the final of a series of instructional steps, according to the pedagogy of German philosopher Johann Friedrich Herbart (1776–1841), based on the inductive empirical method: (a) preparation, that is, review of background knowledge; (b) presentation of new knowledge to be assimilated; (c) assimilation by comparison of the old and new knowledge; (d) generalization, that is, identification of corresponding cases that may integrate the same class of phenomena; and (e) application. The first three steps fit the moment of observation, which is followed by generalization and confirmation (Saviani, 1984). In this model, homework represents the opportunity to test one's own learning through new examples, that is, to apply the new knowledge and confirm assimilation. Application exercises provide opportunity to independently test knowledge and evaluate one's own performance.

The traditional practice of homework as knowledge application, learning confirmation, and self-evaluation by the student, as well as evaluation of the pedagogical process and replanning by the teacher, meant that everyday students handed in homework to be individually reviewed by the teacher out of class. Homework offered teachers the prime and perhaps sole opportunity to identify types and range of difficulties, and evaluate individual and class performance systematically. This used to be the way when I attended elementary school in the 1960s in Brazil, for instance.

Recent transformations in the modes of teaching, related to the *technicization* and *intensification* (Apple, 1985) of work practices, have changed the form of homework evaluation. Current common procedures include: teacher reviews homework orally in class and students make self-corrections; pairs of students exchange and check each other's homework; groups discuss homework *findings*. Teachers do not have time to check individual homework sheets, and often collect them for bureaucratic control purposes since grading is often on completion rather than on correctness. While teachers often seem to spend more time planning instruction and reporting assessments, informal evaluation has been reduced mainly to class time. As a result, both in the U.S. and in Brazil, I have found that the typical 50-minute class consists of the teacher reviewing past homework, briefly presenting new content (or demonstrating a procedure, or assigning a reading), handing out new homework, explaining and discussing instructions, and motivating the students to do it at home. Thus, *homework may occupy the whole class.*

There are, of course, alternatives to routine application homework. In fact, the conception and practice of homework is likely to vary across student age and grade, and content and task nature and purpose. In my own experience as a student, for instance, from middle school on, homework mostly meant *study on your own.* According to current constructivist methods, homework may be designed to fit the moments of observation and generalization in the model previously described. It can be conceived as an aid to cooperative learning (Foyle, Lyman, Tompkin, Perne & Fayle 1990), or as open special projects to be individually or collectively conceptualized and articulated by students, or else as interdisciplinary projects carefully designed by a group of teachers. In such instances, homework provides occasion for nonroutinized practices, therefore involving extra resources and energies of both teachers and students, and frequently of parents as well (Carger & Ayers, 1995).

The link of homework to formal assessment is another significant point. In the traditional instructional model described earlier, homework was evaluated in order to improve instruction and offer individual feedback, but not graded, as grading was left to the moment of exams. Evaluation appeared as formally summative, but it could be really formative, depending on the informal work (actually close homework evaluation) developed by the teacher. Apparently, to minimize the threat of exams, in the name of formative evaluation, or perhaps as a measure of effort intending to countervail plain momentary performance, homework started being graded. In the American public schools attended by my children, from 1993 to 1997, for instance, the typical grade composition was 40% homework, 40% tests, and 20% projects.

But grading homework creates its own difficulties. Here is an example. In December 1996 I received the following *Interim Report of Student Progress* from my 10th-grade son's math teacher: "Valentin has stopped doing his daily work with any regularity. His test scores have been excellent (96%), but his homework (lack of it) will lower his grade." I asked Valentin why he had not been doing his homework, and he answered: "What for if I already know it?" Of course, I pointed at the grade-lowering consequence, and insisted that he had to do the things he did not like as much as those that he liked, but he ended up with a D in math, his favorite subject, and I ended up with no arguments to press him. And because I saw no use in approaching the teacher—because I do not think of my parental role in relation to the school as one of asking the teacher to give my son especial treatment, or as one of teaching the teacher how to do his or her job better—I was probably counted among the negligent parents.

A possible implication of grading homework is to equalize measures of outcomes of students who do homework and perform low in tests and others who do not do homework and perform high in tests, though it is expected that doing homework will generally enhance test performance. Even if homework grading intends to reward effort versus ability, nonetheless what is being assessed is actually *family support*, which is dependent on economic, cultural, and other contingent conditions. Thus, assessing the process of learning and not the outcome is complicated when that process occurs at home, away from the teacher. Within a constructivist practice, for instance, teachers have attempted to assess students' abilities to communicate attempts at solving homework problems. This is just one example of a *solution* that obviously creates new problems.

Implications for Teachers

The first obvious way in which homework affects teachers refers to the variety of possibilities of planning instruction in relations to diverse conceptions of homework—ranging from routine textbook exercises and chapter outlines, followed by quick classroom check up, to creative homework formats requiring close evaluation. Increasing instructional time and articulating additional work developed out of the class requires that teachers design and make explicit some sort of integration. This means more planning and an increase in the amount and complexity of teachers' tasks, the more so when teachers are formally expected to design homework according to students' needs and individual differences, as preached by the best intentioned prohomework rhetoric (e.g., East Lansing Educational Foundation, 1996; Foyle & Lyman, 1989; Ziegler, 1986). The point is that increasing instructional time and extending the spaces of learning also increases teachers' work in planning and evaluation.

But homework also affects teacher work in another, indirect, profound way. Homework has been seen as a "natural means of home–school collaboration" (Olympia et al., 1994), but parents and teachers have also been considered "natural enemies" (Waller, 1965). The literature on teacher–parent relationships is replete with references to silent or overt conflicts, especially in the contexts of social class, ethnic, and language diversity, where apparent lack of support for homework may be common. Even in more homogeneous middle-class contexts, precisely the kind in which parents are expected to collaborate, there are tensions between teachers and "pushy, professional parents" (Biklen, 1995, p. 131); furthermore, teachers especially resent mothers' interference in the classroom as a "challenge to their professional identity" (p. 139). Generally, parental involvement in schools involves issues of power, authority, and control over curricular goals, instructional methods, assessment, resources, decision making and accountability (Fine, 1993).

Two contradictions might best illustrate the strategic and dangerous role of homework within the complicated school–family educational partnership. First, because schoolwork is sent home and often requires some kind of parental work, parents become, at the same time, subordinated to school dictates and empowered (in the role of collaborators and, somehow, insiders) to charge teachers and schools. Parents become the targets of specific meetings, workshops, contracts, guides, manuals, packages, checklists, and letters especially designed to make the home–school connection and to teach them certain instructional tasks (e.g., Association of American Publishers, 1989; Gallagher, 1994; Mafnas et al. 1993; Orman, 1993), whereby teachers come to share some pedagogical knowledge with nonprofessionals. As parents are pressed to learn pedagogy according to the school's curricular agenda, by telling parents what to do, teachers lose some of their exclusive expertise and, thus, are disempowered.

Second, insofar as families provide resources and learning opportunities, school operational costs might decrease, but teachers' gains seem doubtful. Because schoolwork is sent home, and the parents are assigned pedagogical responsibilities and specific instructional tasks, becoming explicitly accountable for the school achievement of their children, teachers consequently become less accountable by formally sharing obligations and accountability with families. Students' failure, then, may be more authoritatively attributed to negligent families and lack of homework.

But issues of accountability between school and family regarding learning outcomes still reflect on teacher professional status in complex ways. Rieck (1994), for instance, suggested a *more realistic* way of assessing high school teachers' performance: to adopt an "adjusted failure rate" encompassing student-caused failures, namely absence and incomplete homework. In this way, teachers would be liberated from an onus, but certainly would lose latitude regarding their specific power, that is, the power to teach effectively and prevent students' failure.

Implications for Parents

My own experience offers a different cultural perspective on expectations about schooling and homework. In Brazil, students attend school for half a day—a period of 4 hours, at the most. (Due to economic reasons, that is, maximization of physical resources, even the private schools offer at least two daily shifts.) In that context, the routine of middle- and upper-class students includes homework and a variety of extracurricular courses led by full-time mothers or private tutors. Unfortunately, students from poor and working-class families are often expected (by middle-class teachers, although not yet by formal policy) to fit the tutored homework routine model. Yet, the critique that school learning is insufficient in terms of time and deficient in terms of quality is especially targeted at the public schools.

Brazilian educators and parents would like to have a *full-time school*, with 8 hours of daily attendance and good quality education. Common sense suggests that, then, homework will not need to be assigned, thus liberating parents and students. Teachers would also benefit as they would have more time to teach a richer curriculum, without depending on family resources. Within this logic, it is interesting to note that *alternative* (progressive) private schools in Brazil compete for their middle-class clientele based on the argument that, because they offer a higher quality education, they do not demand homework. "Your child will learn everything he or she needs to learn here," they advertise, disguising the fact that they count on a rich cultural and academic home curriculum, due to their selected clientele.

In contrast, in the United States, the rhetoric of parental involvement not only has posed homework as a moral obligation, but also has blurred the distinction between homework and leisure, as parents are expected to make enthusiastic efforts to help children with homework assignments. As Hoover-Dempsey and Sandler (1997) suggested, this is part of the very cultural definition of the parental role. Yet, contradictorily, at the same time that too much is expected from home education, too little recognition seems to be granted to the real homework of parents. It is as if the benefits of homework were just derived from student independent performance, as suggested by the U.S. Secretary of Education research-based advice:

> Effective homework assignments do not just supplement the classroom lesson; they also *teach students to be independent learners* [italics added]. Homework gives students experience in following directions, making judgments and comparisons, raising additional questions for study, and developing responsibility and self-discipline. (U.S. Department of Education, 1987, p. 53)

To be sure, it is not the homework *assignment* that gives students all those benefits, but the *experience* that takes place in the home environment, assisted by the parents. Hence, if the home is expected to be the setting of effective homework and all the learning outcomes just stated, the home-schoolers then might know better.

Indeed, according to Bowditch (1993), the current pro-homework movement has been enforcing a curious division of labor between teachers and families:

> Teachers have been charged primarily, either implicitly or explicitly, with the limited tasks of *presenting information* and *covering material*; families, which most often means mothers, have been assigned the tasks of *motivating* students and providing the time, space, and extracurricular attention or assistance to ensure that *learning* takes place. (p. 178)

Yet, insofar as the conditions of implementation and accomplishment of the goals established by homework policies depend on the home and family conditions, it is imperative to consider the parents' perspective. In fact, parental agreement on the value of homework has been taken for granted, as attested by the existence of a few studies on this issue (e.g., Belmont Elementary School District, 1983; Featherstone, 1985; Rose, 1994).

What do parents need in order to get involved and actually monitor homework? The first condition is obviously to have free time. Another condition is to know how, which includes knowing subject matter content and pedagogy. But another basic condition is will and liking. Very few parents hold all three.

Creating learning opportunities in the home, according to school prescriptions, demands time from parents in order to organize and continually adapt the home environment to fit school demands. Parents know what it means to *help* interpret and review homework, to arrange and assist after school and weekend group-homework meetings, and to provide materials not found around the house, among other forms of support. Although families basically exist for children, they have their own needs, obligations, and policies (goals and practices), including children's house chores, sleep time, and family activities (not family math!), with which school homework interferes.

Regarding the second condition, it is reasonable to question whether parents should be taught to monitor homework. Would this *extra* investment in homework workshops not be better applied to teachers and schools, instead? Every parent who glances at homework knows that he or she cannot simply draw on his or her own knowledge and previous school experience: Contents and methods of instruction keep changing, and so do homework formats. Moreover, tutoring homework implies deciphering instructions and expectations posed by a teacher with whom the parent is not in daily contact; hence a natural problem of communication and the "homework assistance telephone service" solution, a curious example of school investment in homework.

Every parent also knows that a very small part of the school curriculum has actually served him or her throughout life (e.g., Connell, Ashenden, Kessler, & Downsett, 1982). Thus, regarding the third condition, is it reasonable to expect all parents to choose to invest their free time in learning the school curriculum again in order to help their children? Would schooling be so appealing for adults who would wish an update, or else would still wish access in case they were not schooled in their time?

Two rhetorical strategies seem to address this problem. The first is simply (but pervasively) expressed by the moral appeal embedded in the discourse of children's school success versus failure, often related to the appeal at parents' sharing their children's school experiences. In this light, homework is even pictured as an opportunity to build parent–child closeness. The second refers to the curricular attempt to link school knowledge and everyday knowledge. As an illustration of school expectations of parental involvement, Michigan's *Programs for Educational Opportunity* (1995) offered *Family Math* and *Family Science* workshops aimed at "helping parents and children learn about mathematics and science together," using "materials and situations that are commonly found around the house." Through this ingenious strategy, homes become classrooms, parents simultaneously become teachers and students, and child education merges with adult education. And, as it is stated, it is supposed to be *fun*!

In summary, prohomework discourses have encompassed two conceptions and possibilities: *home-learning activities*, intentionally involving parents, and activities that students can perform independently. But parents know well that independence is a long, gradual process and that most students cannot perform without help.

Finally, the conditions just stated point at a particular family model— one that counts on an adult (usually the mother) with free time, knowledge, and an especial disposition to educate children. Indeed, if the family can be conceived as "America's smallest school" (Barton & Coley, 1992), it is because it has counted on a dedicated mother. As school has counted on female teachers as cheap workforce in the past, housework, childcare, and also school homework have depended on free, donated mothers' work, burdening additionally those women who work for a pay or outside the home. Hence, a feminist claim against homework.

As Bowditch (1993) argued, it is obvious that "the rhetoric of parental involvement . . . assumes, legitimates, and seeks to enforce a particular normative model of the family—a model . . . that has become decreasingly representative of American families across socioeconomic classes" (p. 179), as the numbers of single-parent families and working mothers have been significantly expanding. Thus, it is critical to acknowledge that through the homework policy "schools make heavy demands on the organization of family life and the practices of mothers, which given recent changes in family structure, may no longer be reasonable" (p. 178). (As for the fact that fathers also may help with homework, it does not invalidate the claim that homework burdens family life.)

Whereas the homework policy both subordinates parents to school mandates and charges them with a cost, that is, extra work, an additional perverse effect, as Bowditch (1993) pointed out, is that by "teaching families their 'basic obligations' to provide the appropriate home environment for learning," school policy creates the conditions for "blaming families for their inadequacies and then retreating from the responsibility to teach the children of those families" (p. 179). This is a clear threat exactly to the children of low-income, working-class, ethnic minority and, especially, working-mother families.

Equity and Accountability

In my view, homework is the key issue within the effective home–school partnership. Its purpose is to promote more and better learning, through "home-based reinforcement of school behavior" (Fullan, 1991), that is, parental tutoring. By acknowledging and drawing on the home as an important factor of school achievement, the homework policy attributes the responsibility of school success or failure to kids and their families (McCaslin & Good, 1992). In this sense, homework is fundamentally a political issue as much as a cultural issue. In France, for instance, homework was prohibited since the 1968 reforms (Weitz, 1977), and there has been notice of at least one attempt to make homework compulsory in a U.S. school board (Thompson, 1978).

To illustrate, there was a recent claim at "abolishing homework" posed by school board member Garrett Redmond, from Half Moon Bay, California, as reported by Gill and Schlossman (1995). Redmond's arguments were that homework (a) "threatened family life, depriving children of quality time with their parents;" and (b) "was unfair because many children lacked the computers, encyclopedias, and quiet places enjoyed by more fortunate students" (p. B7). Gill and Schlossman (1995) counterargued that "homework is parent's eyes and ears" (p. B7). It is the "primary, often the sole communication link that informs parents about the school's academic mission," opening "an otherwise closed window to the school's intellectual agenda" (p. B7). Furthermore, it "compels teachers to let parents see what they are doing in the classroom and how well they are doing their job" (p. B7).

Redmond expressed both points of view of the parents who have time and material resources to invest in homework but have other preferences about family lifestyle, and of the parents who lack those resources. His first concern was about quality of parent–child interactions, since homework usurps the space and time of leisure. His second concern was equity, since homework is part of the measure of student success or failure in school and further social life.

Gill and Schlossman's (1995) arguments addressed the political necessity of evaluating a public service, in terms of content and quality of education that is offered to youngsters, and teacher accountability. As part of the implicit *educational contract* between family and school, the family should supervise and intervene in the educational process, besides participating in the very definition of educational policy. However, the evaluation of public education constitutes more than a family concern, transcending individual families' interests. In fact, democratic participatory evaluation of public services is a complex issue in its own right, related to the organization of social systems and everyday life.

The dispute over the harms and benefits of homework invite other questions related to institutional functions and roles of schools and teachers, and families and parents. Should subject matter learning (the transmission of a certain, historically constructed, body of disciplinary knowledge) be temporally and spatially confined to school or should it have a place at home? My own view, as a mother and as a teacher, is that (within present social organization) subject matter instruction (along with public ethics) is the *specific* function of the school and the professional role of teachers, while domestic education, ideally including physical, affective, and moral aspects, is *mainly* the function of the family. However, this distinction is considerably blurred in current educational policy, at both discourse and practice levels. It is interesting to notice how often teachers complain about the omission of parents regarding problems of student discipline in the school (viewed as moral flaws), and how extensively schools have offered drug prevention programs and parenting skills workshops, as if families were not performing their basic educative function. Contradictorily, at the same time in which schools have extended their function in psychosocial development, encompassing previous familial functions, families have been pressed to do the intellectual training of the students through the homework policy. It is a curious exchange.

Are parents entitled to closely assist intellectual development? This is, in my account, a specialized practice, precisely a profession. Are teachers capable of assisting the psychosocial and moral development of numerous and diverse students? Within the present school mode of organization, this is an impossible task. Families and schools are distinct social institutions and one cannot substitute for the other. Although schools are ideally *learning communities* and a privileged site of training for collective life within democratic principles, they cannot solve or even minimize the so-called *crisis of the family*. So, considering their concrete limitations, when schools invest more in psychosocial goals, they end up investing less in their specific academic goals. Conversely, when parents are compelled to invest time in the intellectual training of their children, they obviously have less time to take care of their other needs, including other kinds of education. Without doubt, the image of the family as "America's smallest school" (Barton & Coley, 1992) is quite gloomy from an affective point of view.

Of course, learning in general, and subject matter learning in particular, are not confined to school. But the school, as a specialized institution, should focus on the learning that occurs within its boundaries and assess solely the learning constructed within classroom practices. This is obviously an enormous task. For those who advocate the legitimacy and desirability of parental involvement in academic learning, the fact that all homes do not hold the conditions to help with homework should be just as obvious (Ivey, 1988). Because most homes do not hold the conditions in order to actively support the school curriculum, the equity goal of education is radically undermined.

Moreover, when Gill and Schlossman (1995) suggested that families should be the guardians of the content and quality of the schooling provided their children, they presented the view of educational researchers, who are qualified to assess school practices. In contrast, most parents cannot perform such a role for the same basic reasons they cannot assist with homework: lack of specialized knowledge, and lack of time to learn how to evaluate instruction.

The issue of democratic participation—confused within the rhetoric of consumer choice—is a thorny one. It is currently at stake in both the parental involvement and school choice policies, which stress freedom and opportunity, promising direct consumer control, school accountability, and recovery of the quality of the public school. However, insofar as parental participation and choice basically require free time and expertise in order to evaluate school performance, differentiation in the quality of schooling is likely to persist, as a result of differentiation in the conditions of the parents.

The possibility that parents evaluate teachers' performance is also a delicate issue. In front of parents, teachers are experts and hold the competent discourse, which may be used to silence less educated parents. In turn, teachers often feel pressured and threatened by certain (too involved) parents' suspicion and demands. The ideal, but not the rule, is that family and school share the same *mission*, so that teacher–parent relationships may flow conveniently. Antagonism between teachers and parents may emerge based on mutual prejudices, but may be masked because there is a child or a job at stake. Although research indicates that parents are willing to get involved with children's schoolwork and would welcome specific guidance from teachers (Dauber & Epstein, 1993; U.S. Department of Education, 1987), such findings are doubtful on the grounds that parents, when inquired directly (and being implicitly evaluated as parents), tended to confirm school expectations, general ideas about good parenting, and the conventional moral obligations related to their children's success in school.

THE REARTICULATION OF HOME AND SCHOOL

Homework appears as a camp of expression of multiple goals related to academic achievement, character development, and even *family cohesion* (Gill & Schlossman, 1995). On the one hand, homework is pictured as necessary and enjoyable. Current definitions of homework focus on "a positive social interaction with parents with gradually increasing independent responsibilities" (Speaker, 1990, p. 57). Especially at the elementary level, "interactive homework *helps* parents and children come together on activities they *enjoy*" (Epstein, 1994, p. 17). Homework kits are defined as "*leisure* time activities" (Ward, 1993, p. 31). And yet, homework has required formal enforcement. School districts have developed explicit homework guidelines regulating amount, length, and kind of homework assignments, number of week nights, grading practices, and parental roles (Roderique et al. 1994; Rose, 1994), in addition to a number of parent guides to help with homework in different school disciplines that have recently been published (Gallagher, 1994). Teachers send homework contracts to be signed by the parent (Mafnas et al., 1993), require daily parental feedback on students' journals (Wisdom, 1993), or send questionnaires related to specific homework assignments to be answered by the parent.

This movement toward family educational accountability can be interpreted in terms of a redefinition of the scope and functions of schooling within cultural politics, as a movement that extends the reach of the school and its knowledge (the dominant culture and its current forms of science and technology) in order to encompass domestic education and community cultural life. Through the formalization of homework within the family–school partnership, educational policy is regulating family life and sociocultural life, an interesting case of extending the *disciplinary power* (Foucault, 1977) of the school to children's homes and to parenting activities. Thus, homework becomes a case of family education and cultural politics. Only within this framework can the TV versus homework polemic, for instance, persistently hold the attention of school educators.

School has become a mediator between individual, family, and diverse (popular) cultures, on one side, and socioeconomic structures, formal (dominant) culture, and public life, on the other. Homework, academic learning, family, and school cannot be considered apart from the power relations that shape social life. In the present state of social relations, it seems that families and students have little power in shaping educational policies, such as homework and the content and direction of instruction. In fact, the practice of developing schoolwork in the home and influencing school policy has been historically restricted to the middle classes. Evaluation of instructional policies and reforms have not counted with broad family input, even though educational policy generally depends on *social consent* as a condition for successful implementation. What is noteworthy, however, is that homework as a formal policy imposes sanctions and, thus, discriminates particular individuals and groups positively or negatively, hence its political character.

As a complex social, moral, and political enterprise, education should never be entirely encompassed and directed by the school. School provides a specific kind of education, socially necessary, but limited. The family offers a distinct educative realm and should recover its role in education, which of course depends primarily on improved material conditions for the majority of families. It is desirable that distinct educative realms, groups, and communities provide for diversity in both individual development and social life. Contrary to the idea of a *close* (formally regulated) school–family partnership, I claim that *gaps*, such as those between school and family, may represent much needed spaces of freedom and creativity in social life.

Rethinking the Impact of Homework on School Achievement

My argument admits that homework does have an impact on school achievement. As an institutionalized practice implying direct grading and increased learning time also assessed by other instruments such as testing, homework may generate positive or negative results. The issue is not simply that homework intends to help raise learning and achievement—it is that if a student does not succeed in homework per se, his or her chances of succeeding in school are already undermined.

Furthermore, homework is not likely to help at-risk students, because it requires the same favorable socioeconomic conditions at home, that those students basically need to succeed in school, anyhow. As a strategy to intensify learning, held at the expense of the family, homework depends on family conditions and, thus, may enhance the chances of failure it intends to reduce. As a compensatory policy for schools' insufficiencies, it may well magnify the problem. This is possible because it affects the instructional practices carried in the classroom, the proper place where the learning of the school curriculum should be intensified.

As an instrument linking family and school toward certain common (but restricted) educational goals, homework imposes the academic curriculum on family life and, by using family time and resources, subordinates families to school. Moreover, as a particular expression of educational policy, homework subjects the educational values of the family to the purposes of school achievement, as well as to the prevailing concepts of individual success and national triumph.

Rethinking the Impact of Homework on Family Life

Whenever I read or hear claims about the desirability of homework and the natural obligation of parents to be homework helpers, I think to myself that these homework acolytes either do not have children, are not the parents of many children or of children who do not enjoy homework, perhaps they raised their children a long time ago before certain curricular reforms, are men who counted or count on a dedicated full-time wife–mother, are teachers who also enjoy teaching at home, or they are super-parents, whom I do not envy.

Thus, it was with satisfaction that I found Corno's (1996) recognition that *homework is a complicated thing,* and Natriello's (1997) *hoist on the petard of homework,* a researcher's penitence on the homework prescription. Natriello found out for himself about the "incredible homework burden," the family evenings "lost to homework," all of it intensified by "challenging" homework assignments provided by a "serious" teacher (pp. 572–573). As an enthusiast of constructivist approaches and higher-order learning, and in a two parent-two children family situation, he thus assessed the parent–homework fit:

> The assignments seem to be a good mix of tasks that vary across subject areas and from routine review to creative exploration. Both kinds of assignments pose challenges to parents. The routine tasks sometimes carry directions that are difficult for two parents with only advanced graduate degrees to understand, and we are forced to rely on our children, who seem to have better intuition about how to read such directions. . . . More creative homework tasks are a mixed blessing on the receiving end. . . . they require one to be well rested, a special condition of mind not often available to working parents. . . . At my house the fancy carriage of constructivism turns into the pumpkin of didactism sometime between 8:30 and 9:00 pm. (Natriello, 1997, p. 573)

It is all the more important to observe that his lament over not spending "the remainder of the school year in quiet evenings of contemplation, sherry, and poetry" (p. 574) does not correspond to the picture of family life of most working parents, although his time constraints and difficulties in helping his children with homework are certainly points in common among parents of all social classes and circumstances.

Epilogue

Perverse Effects of Parental Involvement as Policy: Extending Symbolic Violence to the Realm of the Family and Weakening the Egalitarian Ideal of Public Education

In this volume I inquire about parental involvement in schooling, and particularly in academic learning, as a model for family–school relations and as a strategy to enhance and equalize educational outcomes. Knowing (from my own experience in a distinct social context) about the various problematic aspects of both parental involvement and distance from school—which seem unequivocally related to social class culture and concrete meanings (and rewards) of schooling, the general social selective function of the educational system, the objective and subjective conditions of families, parents, and students, and the interactions between family needs and the quality of school services, within specific and changing social arrangements— I seek to understand the historical origins and cultural meanings of this policy, the ways in which it has been sustained by educational policy discourses and by the specific instructional practice of homework, and especially what effects it might produce in the context of U.S. education.

A historical view of the construction of public schooling reveals an original project both distinct from family education and akin to democratic ideals. Notwithstanding, schools have played a specific part in the reproduction of social hierarchies within social, economic, and cultural change, by grossly converting individual, gender, family, ethnic, and class conditions into unequal educational achievement. In this process, a history of successful schooling and social rewards (for instance, upward social mobility) was constructed, including ideologies like meritocracy and practices (politics) like parental involvement.

Accordingly, the call for parental involvement in education appeals to powerful cultural meanings and typical sentiments and values related to family fulfillment, strength, cohesion, and obligation, but also to individual initiative, competition, and search for advantage, exemplified by current phrases such as *constructing the school career, obtaining a tailored education,* and *negotiating the school system* in order to get the best opportunities for one's child. In constructing the role of the school as one of offering opportunities that individuals (students and their families) may use for their own advancement, this policy is blind to both the external social function and internal workings of the educational system within the process of reproduction of social inequality, as well as to the limits of the logic of educational opportunity. Thus, it inevitably produces negative effects: students shortcomings can be attributed to lack of parental involvement, family apathy in front of the school's implicit and explicit demands can be addressed as cultural deficit, and the meaning of education can be constructed in terms of individual responsibility and family choice, omitting social responsibility.

The fact that schools have limited power to transform social conditions, and have not succeeded in fostering a common (and high) level of individual development or in equalizing basic educational outcomes, does not mean that schools' relative power—the very power of social reproduction proper of any education, which has been used by modern school to reproduce social hierarchies in new ways—should not be preferably and persistently directed toward the purpose of democratic equality. Unfortunately, at this moment, the sway of the neo-liberal political agenda is placing accountability fully on the individual, blaming disadvantaged groups as a result. In educational policy, the formalization of parental involvement—along with other reforms like school choice, and the instructional stress on autonomous and more accountable learners—represents just one aspect of the current retraction of public responsibility, supposedly on behalf of individual, family, and community empowerment. In this way, the current policy rhetoric clearly admits that schools have no power, or that their power is subordinate to the family:

> The effective functioning of schools has depended on the effective functioning of the family and community. What makes some ghetto schools function poorly is that the communities and families they serve are weak, lacking the social capital that would reinforce the school's goals. (Coleman, 1991, p. 13)

The fact that family input has come to be formally recognized as an essential condition for school effectiveness reveals the betrayal of the democratic project of public education: a school devised to be effective independently from, and precisely in order to counterbalance, unequal social conditions that harm individuals and hinder their development.

The (direct or indirect) role of the family in student achievement is indisputable: By preparing children to adapt and succeed in school by developing literate, school-like practices at home and further backing the school curriculum (conveying and incrementing cultural capital), and by participating in school events and developing close connections with school staff in order to exert influence on behalf of their children (investing social capital), middle- and upper-class parents (and occasionally low-class and minority parents) mediate their children's school performance. The selective function of school is also undeniable: Its curriculum counts on a certain family cultural background and continual support, and its practices build on daily home, specifically academic, workings. The fact that teachers expect more from students who have involved parents (because those students are more likely to respond and corroborate their efforts) tells about the importance of symbolic exchanges in the production of school outcomes. And it also tells of where and with whom resides the ultimate power of reproduction within schooling—in the school's cultural (i.e., arbitrary) standards, and with the teachers.

Thus, the family–school partnership means that families invest their cultural and social capital, while schools capitalize on specific forms of capital (already unevenly available in society), sanctioning their conversion into academic capital, that is, grades and credentials. Accurately, there can be no academic partnership for school success in the case of those families who do not possess the required symbolic capital. At the same time, partnership in school governance tends to be concretely limited. As a result, those families and groups who can seize the opportunity to participate in school governance might use it in detriment to the interests of those less powerful. Hence, the degree of success of this policy, in terms of benefiting all students, or those most in need, tends to be limited from the outset. However, while it is very likely that family–school relations will just remain as they are, with low levels of parental involvement, schools will have a lever to tighten their selective function, discriminating between students of positively involved and noninvolved parents. Effects on the development of instruction are also conceivable, the most obvious being the likely scenario in which teachers' efforts at communicating with parents and helping them enhance their parenting efficacy will drain energy away from classroom processes.

From the perspective of the family, the immediate implication of more parental involvement is a demand for time, and also for specific social and intellectual skills. In this way, the so-called opportunity to participate is likely to be perceived as an extra burden by precisely those parents who have not been involved because of lack of time and/or skills. Moreover, the mandate on particular kinds of involvement basically restricts families' choices regarding private life, supposedly in the name of benefiting their children, hence imposing a strong moral sanction. The imposition of parental tutoring of children's school homework, for instance, is set to engage the parents in home tasks prescribed by the school instead of in other educational and leisure activities of their choice.

One interesting question related to the formalization of parental involvement is whether by making explicit the (previously implicit) contribution of the family (to be sure, a limited number of families) to school achievement this policy would really create opportunity and, consequently, increment family input precisely where it is found lacking. Notwithstanding, it is very doubtful that a formal incentive drawing basically on individual (parental) motivation and effort can create the conditions to overcome objective and subjective impediments present in the family and broader social contexts, as well as in parent–teacher relations, so that all families become educationally productive in the terms defined by the school. It is also implausible that schools should carry a massive effort at parent re-education toward this goal.

A question remains: Why the current stress on family educational accountability? One possible answer addresses the limits of schools in promoting both education and social equalization. In this case, shared accountability helps spare schools and teachers the recurrent rhetoric of blame for the social crisis, while simultaneously diverting attention from school problems. Along this line, the need for parental involvement can be read contradictorily as both acknowledgement of the weakness of school, and the set up of a new scapegoat.

Considering that parental re-education is a necessary requirement of parental involvement, another answer bears upon the very cultural project of schooling within the social order—its central role in the reproduction of the dominant cultural arbitrary and social hierarchies, in Bourdieu and Passeron's (1977) terms, or its role in building and maintaining the cultural hegemony of the dominant classes, in Gramsci's (1979) terms—via the reinforcement of meritocracy (and its related values and practices, such as individual effort, and student assessment), and via the legitimization of a certain kind of education and the dissemination of up-to-date knowledges and technologies. In this sense, parental involvement legitimates the whole project and practices of schooling, as well as the cultural practices furthered through schooling (e.g., the current use of computers), and thus can be seen as a consensus building strategy within adult, informal, and continual education.

And, indeed, parental involvement and, particularly, its segment of parent education, have been announced as a timely strategy to *help* minorities who "suffer disproportionately from inadequate education, unemployment, and other social and economic handicaps" (Chavkin, 1993, p. 1), at a moment in which growth in immigration and minority population are amply acknowledged and feared as threats to the domestic economy, the social order, and the national security—hence as a strategy to secure the cultural and linguistic hegemony and promote social efficiency, as it happened a century ago. The implementation of programs like *Family Math* and *Family Science* (Programs for Educational Opportunity, 1995), for instance, suggests a picture in which all families (but especially those in need of exercising these particular discourses) are talking math and science around the dinner table, practicing the language of power at the expense of other languages and cultural expressions.

Thus, the intensification of the cultural hegemony and ideological consensus-building role of schooling by calling on parental involvement, in this case, is bound to stir a host of contradictions. Whereas successful family–school partnerships depend on convergence of views on purposes and contents of education, it is notable that the call for parental involvement has not been coupled with a call to discuss public education, the academic curriculum, and its practices in the school buildings. Moreover, partnerships also depend on agreement over teaching and parenting roles and rights, another polemic arena (Education Week, on-line). And, finally, they require trust and respect between teachers and parents, based not only on common values and goals, but on actual student learning and satisfactory formal outcomes (grades!), which makes it unlikely that precisely those parents of at-risk students will become involved, in spite of happy exceptions.

In this context, the most important political-practical implication of understanding the meaning of education as symbolic violence and the articulation of school and family in social reproduction is the strengthening of the democratic role of the public school, while simultaneously restraining the reach of policy onto private life. On the one hand, symbolic violence or cultural imposition may be tolerable, to some degree, if confined to the public realm, as long as the private sphere bears freedom. On the other hand, schools can only counteract the reproduction of social inequality by extending their pedagogic autonomy in order to produce a common and meaningful experience, and effective and fair outcomes, *precisely through the kinds of teaching and learning generally unavailable at home, and particularly unavailable in many homes.* This requires, fundamentally, commitment to public education, the recovery of democratic ideals, and the specific development of a pedagogy that does not require family input.

I was once provocatively asked whether I was against parental involvement in schooling, that is, if, by recognizing it as a passive or active source of unequal educational outcomes, I would propose that educational policy should better and exactly inhibit it. My answer is that I can neither find fault in parents' interest in their children's education and school success, nor favor parental involvement in schooling as a state policy mandating that all parents be involved. While I cannot find a policy that either obliges or proscribes individual initiative legitimate, I do see the role of the democratic state as one of offering equal opportunities while compensating for unequal social conditions.

References

Abercrombie, N., Hill, S., & Turner, B. S. (1994). *Dictionary of sociology* (3rd ed.). London: Penguin Books.

Anyon, J. (1981). Social class and school knowledge. *Curriculum Inquiry, 11*, 3–42.

Apple, M. W. (1985). Teaching and women's work: A comparative historical and ideological analysis. *Teachers College Record, 86*, 458–466.

Arbanas, R. J. (1994). *Girls + math + science = choices. A handbook for parents*. Marshall, MI: Calhoun Intermediate School District.

Arendt, H. (1961). The crisis in education. *Between past and future: Six exercises in political thought*. New York: Meridian.

Association of American Publishers. (1989). *Helping your child succeed in school*. New York: Author.

Baker, D. P., & Stevenson, D. L. (1986). Mothers' strategies for children's school achievement: Managing the transition to high school. *Sociology of Education, 59*, 156–166.

Barton, P. E., & Coley, R. J. (1992). *America's smallest school: The family*. Princeton, NJ: Educational Testing Service. Policy Information Center. (ERIC Document Reproduction Service N: ED349320)

Becher, R. M. (1984). *Parent Involvement: A review of research and principles of successful practice*. Washington, DC: National Institute of Education.

Belmont Elementary School District. (1983). *Homework surveys for teachers, parents, and students*. Belmont, CA: Author. (ERIC Document Reproduction Service N: ED233464)

Benson, C. S., Medrich, A. E., & Buckley, S. (1980). Families as educators: Time use contributions to school achievement. In J. Guthrie (Ed.), *School finance policy in the 1980s: A decade of conflict* (pp. 169–207). Cambridge, MA: Ballinger.

Berger, B. (1985). The fourth R: The repatriation of the school. In J. H. Bunzel (Ed.), *Challenge to American schools: The case for standards and values* (pp. 81–96). New York: Oxford University Press.

Berliner, D. C. (1997). Educational psychology meets the Christian right: Differing views of children, schooling, teaching, and learning. *Teachers College Record, 98*, 381–416.

Berliner, D. C., & Biddle, B. J. (1995). *The manufactured crisis: Myths, fraud, and the attack on America's public schools*. Reading, MA: Addison-Wesley.

Bidwell, C. (1991). Families, childrearing, and education. In P. Bourdieu, & J. S. Coleman (Eds.), *Social theory for a changing society* (pp. 189–193). Boulder, CO: Westview Press & New York: Russell Sage Foundation.

Biklen, S. K. (1995). *School work: Gender and the cultural construction of teaching.* New York: Teachers College Press.

Bourdieu, P. (1977). Cultural reproduction and social reproduction. In: J. Karabel, & A. H. Halsey (Eds.), *Power and ideology in education* (pp. 487–511). New York: Oxford University Press.

Bourdieu, P. (1986). The forms of capital. In J. G. Richardson (Ed.), *Handbook of theory and research for the sociology of education* (pp. 241–258). New York: Greenwood Press.

Bourdieu, P., & Passeron, J.-C. (1977). *Reproduction in education, society, and culture.* Beverly Hills, CA: Sage.

Bowditch, C. (1993). Response to Michelle Fine's [ap]parent involvement: Reflections on parents, power, and urban public schools. *Teachers College Record, 95,* 177–181.

Bowles, S., & Gintis, H. (1976). *Schooling in capitalist America.* New York: Basic Books.

Cadzen, C. B. (1988). *Classroom discourse: The language of teaching and learning.* Portsmouth, NH: Heinemann.

Caplan, Nathan, Choy, M. H., & Whitmore, J. K. (1992, February). Indochinese refugee families and academic achievement. *Scientific American,* 36–42.

Carger, C. L., & Ayers, W. (1995). It's just homework: Tales from hell and refreshing alternatives. *Rethinking Schools, 10,* 4, 7.

Casanova, U. (1996). Parent involvement: A call for prudence. *Educational Researcher, 25* (8), 30–32, 46.

Chavkin, N. F. (Ed.). (1993a). *Families and schools in a pluralistic society.* Albany: State University of New York Press.

Chavkin, N. F. (1993b). School social workers helping multi-ethnic families, schools, and communities join forces. In N. F. Chavkin (Ed.), *Families and schools in a pluralistic society* (pp. 217–226). Albany: State University of New York Press.

Cherryholmes, C. H. (1988). *Power and criticism: Poststructural investigations in education.* New York: Teachers College Press.

Chubb, J. E., & Moe, T. M. (1990). *Politics, markets, and America's schools.* Washington, DC: The Brookings Institution.

Church, R. L., & Sedlak, M. W. (1976). *Education in the United States.* New York: The Free Press.

Cibulka, J. J., & Kritek, W. J. (Eds.). (1996). *Coordination among schools, families, and communities: Prospects for educational reform.* Albany: State University of New York Press.

Clark, R. M. (1983). *Family life and school achievement: Why poor black children succeed or fail.* Chicago: University of Chicago Press.

Clark, R. M. (1990, Spring). Why disadvantaged students succeed: What happens outside school is critical. *Public Welfare,* 17–23.

Clark, R. M. (1993). Homework-focused parenting practices that positively affect student achievement. In N. F. Chavkin (Ed.). *Families and schools in a pluralistic society* (pp. 85–105). Albany: State University of New York Press.

Cochran, M., & Henderson, C. R., Jr. (1986). *Family matters: Evaluation of the parental empowerment program.* Ithaca, NY: Cornell University Press.

Coleman, J. S. (1966). Equal schools for equal students? *Public Interest, 4,* 70–75.

Coleman, J. S. (1967). Toward open schools. *Public Interest, 9*, 20–27.

Coleman, J. S. (1987). Families and schools. *Educational Researcher, 16*, 32–38.

Coleman, J. S. (1991). *Parental involvement in education* (Order No. 065-000-00459-3). Washington, DC: U.S. Government Printing Office.

Coleman, J., Campbell, E., Hobson, C., McPartland, J., Mood, A., Weinfeld, F., & York, R. (1966). *Equality of educational opportunity report.* Washington, DC: U.S. Government Printing Office.

Connecticut State Department of Education. (1984). *Attendance, homework, promotion and retention: A manual on policy development and administrative procedures.* Hartford, CT: Author. (ERIC Document Reproduction Service N: ED265668)

Connell, R. W., Ashenden, D. J., Kessler, S., & Dowsett, G. W. (1982). *Making the difference: Schools, families and social division.* Sydney, Australia: George Allen & Unwin.

Conover, P. J. (1990, April). *Detention as a deterrent for late assignments: A study.* Paper presented at the annual meeting of the American Educational Research Association, Boston, MA. (ERIC Document Reproduction Service N: ED325910)

Coontz, S. (1992). *The way we never were: American families and the nostalgia trap.* New York: Basic Books.

Cooper, H. (1994). *The battle over homework. An administrators guide to setting sound and effective policies.* Thousand Oaks, CA: Corwin Press. (ERIC Document Reproduction Service N: ED376573)

Corno, L. (1996). Homework is a complicated thing. *Educational Researcher, 25* (8), 27–30.

Cravens, H. (1993). Child saving in modern America: 1870s–1990s. In R. Wollons (Ed.), *Children at risk in America: History, concept, and public policy* (pp. 3–31). Albany: State University of New York Press.

Cummins, J. (1986). Empowering minority students: A framework for intervention. *Harvard Educational Review, 56*, 18–36.

Dauber, S., & Epstein, J. (1993). Parents' attitudes and practices of involvement in inner-city elementary and middle schools. In N. F. Chavkin (Ed.), *Families and schools in a pluralistic society* (pp. 53–71). Albany: State University of New York Press.

David, M. E. (1980). *The state, the family, and education.* London: Routledge & Kegan Paul.

David, M. E. (1989). Schooling and the family. In H. A. Giroux, & P. McLaren (Eds.), *Critical pedagogy, the state, and cultural struggle* (pp. 50–65). Albany: State University of New York Press.

de Carvalho, M. E. P. (1989). *O magistério primário como ocupação feminina: Uma análise das representações sociais de professoras primárias da cidade de São Paulo sobre sua prática profissional.* Unpublished master's thesis, Universidade Estadual de Campinas, Brazil.

de Carvalho, M. E. P., & Ramalho, B. L. (1983). A escola, a família e o fracasso escolar. *Educação e Cultura (Brazil), 9* (III).

Delpit, L. (1988). The silenced dialogue: Power and pedagogy in educating other people's children. *Harvard Educational Review, 58*, 280–298.

Dornbusch, S. M., Ritter, P. L., Leiderman, P. H., Roberts, D. F., & Fraleigh, M. J. (1987). The relation of parenting style to adolescent school performance child. *Child Development, 58*, 1244–1257.

Dornbusch, S. M., & Ritter, P. L. (1988). Parents of high school students: A neglected resource. *Educational Horizons, 66*, 75–77.

Doyle, M. A. E., & Barber, B. S. (1990). *Homework as a learning experience. What research says to the teacher* (3rd ed.). Washington, DC: National Education Association. (ERIC Document Reproduction Services N: ED319492)

Eagle, E. (1989, March). *Socioeconomic status, family structure, and parental involvement: The correlates of achievement.* Paper presented at the annual meeting of the American Educational Research Association, San Francisco, CA.

East Lansing Educational Foundation. (1996). *Student agenda, 1996–1997.* East Lansing, MI: East Lansing Public Schools.

Education Week [On-line]. Available: http://www.edweek.org/context/topics/parent.htm.

Elkind, D. (1995). School and family in the postmodern world. *Phi Delta Kappan, 77,* 8–14.

Epps, M. (1966). *Homework.* Washington, DC: National Education Association. (ERIC Document Reproduction Service N: ED017076)

Epstein, J. L. (1991). Effects on student achievement of teachers' practices of parent involvement. *Advances in Reading/Language Research, 5,* 261–276.

Epstein, J. L. (1992). School and family partnerships. In M. Alkin (Ed.), *Encyclopedia of educational research* (6th ed., pp. 1139–1151). New York: MacMillan.

Epstein, J. L. (1993). Foreword. In Swap, S. M. (1993). *Developing home–school partnerships: From concepts to practice* (pp. IX–XII). New York: Teachers College Press.

Epstein, J. L. (1994). School–home connection. Make language arts a family affair. *Instructor, 103,* 17, 22–23.

Epstein, J. L. (1995). School, family, community partnerships: Caring for the children we share. *Phi Delta Kappan, 76,* 701–712.

Epstein, J. L. (1996). Perspectives and previews on research and policy for school, family, and community partnerships. In A. Booth, & J. F. Dunn (Eds.), *Family–school links: How do they affect educational outcomes?* (pp. 209–246). Mahwah, NJ: Lawrence Erlbaum Associates.

Epstein, J. L., & Pinkow, L. (1988). *A model for research on homework based on U.S. and international studies (Report No. 27).* Baltimore, MD: Center for Research on Elementary and Middle Schools. (ERIC Document Reproduction Service N: ED301323)

ERIC Abstracts Data Base. Homework Policy.

Families as Educators Special Interest Group, American Educational Research Association. (1996, Fall). *Families as Educators.*

Featherstone, H. (1985). What does homework accomplish? Principal, 65 (2), 6–7. (ERIC Document Reproduction Service N: EJ328022)

Fehrmann, P. G., Keith, T. Z., & Reimers, T. M. (1987). Home influence on school learning: Direct and indirect effects of parental involvement on high school grades. *Journal of Educational Research, 80,* 330–337.

Fine, M. (1993). [Ap]parent involvement: Reflections on parents, power, and urban public schools. *Teachers College Record, 94,* 682–710.

Foucault, M. (1977). *Discipline and punish: The birth of the prison.* New York: Pantheon.

Foyle, H. C., & Lyman, L. (1989, March). *Homework: Research, policy, and implementation.* Paper presented at the annual meeting of the Association for Supervision and Curriculum Development. Orlando, FL. (ERIC Document Reproduction Service N: ED303919)

Foyle, H., Lyman, L., Tompkin, L., Perne, S., & Fayle, D. (1990). *Homework and cooperative learning: a classroom field experiment.* Emporia, KS: Emporia State University. (ERIC Document Reproduction Service N: ED350285)

Fullan, M. G. (1991). *The new meaning of educational change* (2nd ed.). New York: Teachers College Press.

Gagnon, P. (1995, December). What should children learn? *The Atlantic Monthly,* 65–78.

Gallagher, R. (1994). A parent's guide to helping with homework. *Learning, 22,* 67.

Giddens, A. (1979). *Central problems in social theory.* Berkeley, CA: University of California Press.

Gill, B., & Schlossman, S. (1995, January 24). Homework is a parent's eyes and ears. *LA Times,* B7.

Gillum, R. M. (1977, April). *The effects of parent involvement on student achievement in three Michigan performance contracting programs.* Paper presented at the annual meeting of the American Educational Research Association, New York.

Good, C. V. (1973). *Dictionary of Education* (3rd ed.). New York: McGraw-Hill.

Goodson, B. D., & Hess, R. D. (1975). *Parents as teachers of young children: An evaluative review of some contemporary concepts and programs.* Washington, DC: Bureau of Educational Personnel Development.

Gramsci, A. (1979). *Os intelectuais e a organização da cultura.* Rio de Janeiro, Brazil: Civilização Brasileira.

Grubb, W. N., & Lazerson, M. (1982). *Broken promises: How Americans fail their children.* Chicago: University of Chicago Press.

Guest, A., & Tolnay, S. (1985). Agricultural organization and educational consumption in the U.S. in 1900. *Sociology of Education, 58,* 201–212.

Guinagh, B., & Gordon, I. (1976). *School performance as a function of early stimulation.* Gainesville: Florida University at Gainesville, Institute for Development of Human Resources.

Heath, S. B. (1983). *Ways with words: Language, life, and work in communities and classrooms.* New York: Cambridge University Press.

Henderson, A., & Berla, N. (Eds.). (1994). *A new generation of evidence: The family is crucial to student achievement.* Washington, DC: National Committee for Citizens in Education.

Henry, M. E. (1996). *Parent–school collaboration: Feminist organizational structures and school leadership.* Albany: State University of New York Press.

Hoover-Dempsey, K. V., & Sandler, H. M. (1997). Why do parents become involved in their children's education? *Review of Educational Research, 67,* 3–42.

Hossler, C.-A., Stage, F., & Gallagher, K. (1988). *The relationship of increased instructional time to student achievement. Policy Bulletin N. 1.* Bloomington, IN: Consortium on Educational Policy Studies. (ERIC Document Reproduction Series N: ED298671)

Hunter, J. D. (1991). *Culture wars: The struggle to define America.* New York: Basic Books.

Ingham Intermediate School District, MSU Office of the Provost, The Capital Area Regional Math and Science Center. (1995). *An invitation to sample success: A math/science conference for girls in grade six* (Adult Supplement).

Irvine, D. J. (1979). *Parent involvement affects children's cognitive growth.* Albany: University of the State of New York, State Education Department, Division of Research.

Ivey, J. (1988). No Excuses. *Learning, 16* (9), 88. (ERIC Document Reproduction Service N: EJ375666)

Jackson, A. (1989). *Turning points: Preparing American youth for the 21st century.* Washington, DC: Carnegie Council on Adolescent Development.

Kaestle, C. F. (1983). *Pillars of the Republic: Common schools and American society, 1780–1860.* New York: Hill & Wang.

Keddie, N. (1971). Classroom knowledge. In M. F. D. Young (Ed.), *Knowledge and control* (pp. 133–161). London: Collier Macmillan.

Keith, T. Z., & Cool, V. A. (1992). Testing models of school learning: Effects of quality of instruction, motivation, academic coursework, and homework on academic achievement. *School Psychology Quarterly, 7*, 207–226.

Kellaghan, T., Sloane, K., Alvarez, B., & Bloom, B. S. (1993). *The home environment & school learning: Promoting parental involvement in the education of children.* San Francisco: Jossey-Bass.

Kozol, J. (1991). *Savage inequalities: Children in America's schools.* New York: Crown.

Labaree, D. F. (1997). Public goods, private goods: The American struggle over educational goals. *American Educational Research Journal, 34*, 39–81.

Lamont, M., & Lareau, A. (1988). Cultural capital: Allusions, gaps and glissandos in recent theoretical developments. *Sociological Theory, 6*, 153–168.

Lankton, R. S., & Rasscharet, W. M. (1961). *Survey of policies on homework.* Michigan: Detroit Public Schools. (ERIC Document Reproduction Service N: ED001444)

Lareau, A. (1987). Social class differences in family–school relationships: The importance of cultural capital. *Sociology of Education, 60*, 73–85

Lareau, A. (1993). *Home advantage.* London: The Falmer Press.

Lazar, I., & Darlington, R. B. (1978). *Summary: Lasting effects after preschool.* Ithaca, NY: Cornell University, Consortium for Longitudinal Studies.

Locke, M. S. (1991). *Increasing homework productivity in third grade through on-site supervision.* Ed.D. Practicum, Fort Lauderdale, FL: Nova University.

Los Angeles Unified School District, CA Office of Instruction. (1983). *Parents and schools: A shared responsibility.* Los Angeles: Instructional Publications, Los Angeles Unified School District. (ERIC Document Reproduction Service N: ED287129)

Luksik, P., & Hoffecker, P. H. (1995). *Outcome-based education: The state's assault on our children's values.* Lafayette, LA: Huntington House Publishers.

Mafnas, I., Flis-Calvo, J., & Dionio, S. (1993). A contract for science. *Science Scope, 17*, 45–48.

Mann, H. (1957). Twelfth Annual Report. In L. Cremin (Ed.), *The republic and the school: Horace Mann on the education of free men.* New York: Teachers College Press.

McCaslin, M., & Good, T. L. (1992). Compliant cognition: The misalliance of management and instructional goals in current school reform. *Educational Researcher, 21*, 4–17.

Mehan, H., Hertweck, A., & Meihls, J. L. (1986). *Handicapping the handicapped: Decision making in students' educational careers.* Stanford, CA: Stanford University Press.

Michaels, S. (1986). Narrative presentations: An oral preparation for literacy with first graders. In J. Cook-Gumperz (Ed.), *The social construction of literacy* (pp. 94–116). Cambridge, NY: Cambridge University Press.

Michigan State Board of Education. (1982). *A Position Statement and Resource Guide on Involvement of Parents and Other Citizens in Education.* Michigan: Author.

Montaigne, M. de (1993). *The essays: A selection.* London: Penguin Books. (Original work published 1580).

Mowry, C. (1972). *Investigation of the effects of parent participation in Head Start: Non-technical report.* Washington, DC: Department of Health, Education, and Welfare.

Murphy, B. (1996, October 2). School district to make detention a family affair [On-line]. *Detroit Free Press.* Available: http://www.freep.com/news/education/qparents25.htm

Murphy, J., & Decker, K. (1989). Teachers' use of homework in high schools. *Journal of Educational Research, 82* (5), 261–69. (ERIC Document Reproduction Service N: EJ398447)

National Commission on Excellence in Education. (1983). *A nation at risk: The imperative for educational reform*. Washington, DC: Department of Education.

National Education Goals Panel. (1995). *The national education goals report: Building a nation of learners*. Washington, DC: U.S. Government Printing Office.

National PTA. (1997). *National standards for parent/family involvement programs*. Chicago, IL: Author.

Natriello, G. (1997). Hoist on the Petard of Homework. *Teachers College Record, 98* (3), 572–575.

Oakes, J. (1986). *Keeping track: How schools structure inequality*. New Haven, CT: Yale University Press.

Office of Educational Research and Improvement. (1992). *Meeting goal 3: How well are we doing? Education Research Report*. Washington, DC: Author.

Office of Educational Research and Improvement. (1996). *A checklist for helping your child with homework*. Washington , DC: Author. (ERIC Document Reproduction Service N: ED401045)

Olmsted, P. P., & Rubin, R. I. (1982). Linking parent behaviors to child achievement: Four evaluation studies from the parent education follow through program. *Studies in Educational Evaluation, 8*, 317–325.

Olympia, D. E., Sheridan, S. M., & Jenson, W. (1994). Homework: A natural means of home–school collaboration. *School Psychology Quarterly, 9*, 60–80.

Orman, S. A. (1993). Mathematics backpacks: Making the home–school connection. *Arithmetic Teacher, 40,* 306–308.

Palardy, J. M. (1988). The effect of homework policies on student achievement. *NASSP Bulletin, 72* (507), 14–17. (ERIC Document Reproduction Service N: EJ370262)

Palardy, J. M. (1995). Another look at homework. *Principal, 74* (5), 32–33. (ERIC Document Reproduction Service N: EJ502901)

Popwell, E. P. (1991). *The after school program for school age children* Report. Report No. 13, Vol. 25. Dept. of Research and Evaluation. Atlanta, GA: Atlanta Public Schools. (ERIC Document Reproduction Service N: ED342840)

Programs for Educational Opportunity. (1995). *Family math, family science, playtime is science*. Michigan: University of Michigan, School of Education, folder.

Radin, N. (1972, December). Three degrees of maternal involvement in a preschool program: Impact on mothers and children. *Child Development*, 1355–1364.

Rieck, W. A. (1994). Student failure rate: A different perspective on the problem. *NASSP Bulletin, 78* (565), 69–73. (ERIC Document Reproduction Service N: EA529956)

Rist, R. C. (1970). Student social class and teacher expectations: The self-fulfilling prophecy and ghetto education. *Harvard Educational Review, 40*, 411–451.

Roderique, T. W., Polloway, E. A., Cumblad, C., Epstein, M. H., & Bursuck, W. D. (1994). Homework: A survey of policies in the United States. *Journal of Learning Disabilities, 27*, 481–487.

Rose, A. C. (1994). Homework preferences: Teachers and parents state their opinions. *NASSP Bulletin, 78* (561), 65–75. (ERIC Document Reproduction Service N: EJ481352)

Rumberger, R. W., Ghatak, R., Poulos, G., Ritter, P. L., & Dornbusch, S. (1990). Family influences on dropout behavior in one California high school. *Sociology of Education, 63,* 283–299.

San Mateo County Office of Education. (1983). *Homework policies of San Mateo county school districts*. Redwood City, CA: SMERC Information Center. (ERIC Document Reproduction Service N: ED233463)

Sanders, B. (1995). *A is for ox: The collapse of literacy and the rise of violence in an eletronic age*. New York: Vintage Books.

Sattes, B. D. (1985). *Parent involvement: A review of the literature*. (Occasional Paper No. 021). Charleston, WV: Appalachia Educational Laboratory.

Saviani, D. (1984). *Escola e democracia*. São Paulo, Brazil: Cortez Editora/Autores Associados.

Schutz, A. (1964). The stranger: An essay in social psychology. In: A. Brodersen (Ed.), *Collected Papers II: Studies in Social Theory* (pp. 91–105). The Hague: Nijhoff. (Original work published 1944. In: *American Journal of Sociology 49*, 499–507.)

Scott-Jones, D. (1984). Family influences on cognitive development and school achievement. *Review of Research in Education, 11*, 259–304.

Scott-Jones, D. (1987). Mother-as-teacher in the families of high- and low-achieving low-income black first-graders. *Journal of Negro Education, 56*, 21–34.

Scott-Jones, D. (1993). Families as educators in a pluralistic society. In N. F. Chavkin (Ed.), *Families and schools in a pluralistic society* (pp. 245–254). Albany: State University of New York Press.

Sedlak, M. W., & Schlossman, S. (1985). The public school and social services: Reassessing the progressive legacy. *Educational Theory, 35*, 371–383.

Seeley, D. S. (1993). A new paradigm for parental involvement. In N. F. Chavkin (Ed.), *Families and schools in a pluralistic society* (pp. 229–234). Albany: State University of New York Press.

Smrekar, C. (1996). *The impact of school choice and community: In the interest of families and schools*. Albany: State University of New York Press.

Speaker, R. B., Jr. (1990). Homework to help literacy development: Language arts (parent and educator). *Reading: Exploration and Discovery, 13*, 57–62.

Stevenson, D. L., & Baker, D. P. (1987). The family–school relation and the child's school performance. *Child Development, 58*, 1348–1357.

Stevenson, H. W., & Stigler, J. W. (1992). *The learning gap*. New York: Simon & Schuster.

Swap, S. M. (1993). *Developing home–school partnerships: From concepts to practice*. New York: Teachers College Press.

Thompson, M. (1978). You think politics and religion are touchy topics? Just mention mandatory homework. American School Board Journal, 165 (3), 37–9. (ERIC Document Reproduction Service N: EJ173620)

Thorne, B., & Yalom, M. (Eds.). (1992). *Rethinking the family: Some feminist questions* (Rev. ed.). Boston: Northeastern University Press.

Tyack, D. (1976). Ways of seeing: An essay on the history of compulsory schooling. *Harvard Educational Review, 46*, 355–389.

U.S. Department of Education. (1987). *What works. Research about teaching and learning*. Washington, DC: Author.

Valdes, G. (1996). *Con respeto: Bridiging the distances between culturally diverse families and schools—An ethnographic portrait*. New York: Teachers College Press.

Van Moorlehem, T. (1997, August 25). School doors open for parents to help. Just a little involvement can boost education [On-line]. *Detroit Free Press*. Available: http://www.freep.com/news/education/ qparent25.htm.

Walberg, H. J. (1984, February). Families as partners in educational productivity. *Phi Delta Kappan*, 397–400.

Walberg, H. J., Bole, R. E., & Waxman, H. C. (1980). School-based family socialization and reading achievement in the inner-city. *Psychology in the Schools, 17*, 509–514.

Waller, W. (1965). *The sociology of teaching*. New York: Science Editions.

Ward, A. (1993). Magnets and electricity. *School Science Review, 74*, 31–38.

Weitz, M. C. (1977). Plus ça change ... or inside a French PTA. *French Review, 50* (3), 393–399. (ERIC Document Reproduction Service N: EJ53695)

White, K. R., Taylor, M. J., & Moss, V. D. (1992). Does research support claims about the benefits of involving parents in early intervention programs? *Review of Educational Research, 62*, 91–125.

Williams, R. (1983). *Keywords: A vocabulary of culture and society.* New York: Oxford University Press.

Willis, P. (1977). *Learning to labor: How working class kids get working class jobs.* New York: Columbia University Press.

Wisdom, C. (1993). Growing together: Sharing through homework journals. *Teaching Pre-K-8, 24*, 93–95.

Wong Fillmore, L. (1990). Now or later? Issues related to the early education of minority-group children. In *Early Childhood and Family Education: Analysis and Recommendations of the Council of Chief State School Officers* (pp. 122–145). New York: Harcourt Brace Jovanovich.

Ziegler, S. (1986). *Homework.* Ontario, Canada: Toronto Board of Education. (ERIC Document Reproduction Service N: ED274418)

Ziegler, S. (1987). *The effects of parent involvement on children's achievement: The significance of home–school links.* Ontario, Canada: Toronto Board of Education.

Author Index

A

Abercrombie, N., 50
Alvarez, B., 14–16
Anyon, J., 60
Apple, M. W., 123
Arbanas, R. J., 119
Arendt, H., 41, 53
Ashenden, D. J., 128
Association of American Publishers, 126
Ayers, W., 124

B

Baker, D. P., 14
Barber, B. S., 118, 122
Barton, P. E., 16, 129, 131
Becher, R. M., 13
Belmont Elementary School District, 127
Benson C. S., 15
Berger, B., 21, 24
Berla, N., 5, 10, 12–17, 94
Berliner, D. C., 108, 110
Biddle, B. J., 110
Bidwell, C., 51, 52, 53
Biklen, S. K., 97, 125
Bloom, B. S., 14–16
Bole, R. E., 15
Bourdieu, P., 5, 9, 14, 19, 22–24, 27, 44–
     46, 48, 67–92, 96, 104, 105, 108,
     110–112, 116, 138

Bowditch, C., 127, 129
Bowles, S., 57, 60
Buckley, S., 15
Bursuck, W. D., 18, 119, 120, 132

C

Cadzen, C. B., 60
Campbell, E., 11, 61
Caplan, N., 95
Carger, C. L., 124
Casanova, U., 2, 3, 5,
Chavkin, N. F., 12, 138
Cherryholmes, C. H., 45
Choy, M. H., 95
Chubb, J. E., 102, 119
Church, R. L., 11, 55
Cibulka, J. J., 11, 12
Clark, R. M., 14, 15
Cochran, M., 14
Coleman, J. S., 10, 11, 27, 52, 61–66, 74,
     94, 95, 96, 102, 136
Coley, R. J., 16, 129, 131
Connecticut State Department of
     Education, 118
Connell, R. W., 128
Conover, P. J., 118, 122
Cool, V. A., 119
Coontz, S., 19, 59, 95
Cooper, H., 18, 119

Subject Index

A

Academic capital, 69, 73, 77, 78, 137
Assessment, 25, 41, 92, 94, 112, 115,
    119, 123–125, 131, *see also*
    Evaluation, Tests/testing
    and class–culture inequalities, 87
    portfolios versus exams, 87
    of teachers, 126
    and universal standards, 112

C

Capital, *see also* Cultural capital, Social
    capital, Academic capital
    concept, 70
    conversions, 23, 67, 69–71, 73, 76,
        77, 111, 112, 137
    economic, 70, 72–78, 107
    forms of, 19, 45, 67, 71, 76, 97
    and labor/time, 70–72, 74, 76, 77
    symbolic, 9, 23, 70, 71
Child-rearing/socialization, 15, 48, 49,
    96, 103, 104, 122
Critical–liberatory pedagogy, 92
Coleman Report, 11, 60
Community–school relations, 2, 5, 11,
    16, 43
Compensatory education, 11–13, 20, 23,
    24, 91–93, 102, 112, 118, 119

Conflict/conflicts,
    cultural/class/religious, 36, 56, 59,
        82, 98, 108
    over curriculum control, 19, 30,
        42, 110, 125
    family–school, 2, 20–22, 29, 42,
        98, 99, 111, 121
    among parents, 2, 3, 30
    parent–expert, 3, 35
    parent–teacher, 2, 3, 19, 20, 29,
        33, 38, 98, 109, 125, 131
Cooperative schools, 33
Cultural arbitrary, 23, 44, 70, 78, 79, 82–
    84, 86, 89–93, 100, 101, 110, 112
    dominant–dominated, 79, 80, 82, 85,
        87, 91, 94, 97, 100, 111, 116
Cultural capital, 9, 23–25, 36, 40, 67–77,
    82, 86, 91–93, 97, 107, 111, 136, 137
    and academic qualifications/
        credentials, 67, 69–71, 73,
        76–78, 81
    as the currency of educational
        achievement/school success,
        9, 23, 24
    as distinction, 72
    embodied, 9, 71, 73, 78, 96
    and family/class socialization, 9,
        23, 72, 94, 110
    institutionalized, 71, 73
    labor market value, 73, 76, 82
    objectified, 71–73, 77

T